Twayne's United States Authors Series

Sylvia E. Bowman, *Editor*

INDIANA UNIVERSITY

Frederick Jackson Turner

TUSAS 254

Frederick Jackson Turner

FREDERICK JACKSON TURNER

By JAMES D. BENNETT

Western Kentucky University

TWAYNE PUBLISHERS

A DIVISION OF G. K. HALL & CO., BOSTON

Library of Congress Cataloging in Publication Data

Bennett, James D.
  Frederick Jackson Turner.

port.

138 p

  (Twayne's United States authors series; 254) 21 cm.
  Bibliography: pp. 121–34.
  Includes index.
  1. Turner, Frederick Jackson, 1861–1932.
E175.5.T83B46   973'.07'2024 [B]   74-32112
ISBN 0-8075-7150-6

MANUFACTURED IN THE UNITED STATES OF AMERICA

FOR MY PARENTS

Contents

About the Author

James D. Bennett is a native Kentuckian and received his early education in the public schools of that state. He holds the Bachelor of Arts degree from Centre College of Kentucky, the Master of Arts degree from Texas Christian University, and the Doctor of Philosophy degree from Vanderbilt University. His interest in the West, and particularly in Frederick Jackson Turner, was stimulated by seminars conducted by the late Professor Walter Prescott Webb at the University of Texas.

Bennett is a member of the Western History Association, the Organization of American Historians, the Southern Historical Association, the Filson Club, and Phi Alpha Theta. His articles have appeared in various state and regional historical publications and in collections of readings. He frequently speaks to historical groups on local and United States history. He has conducted workshops in the teaching of history in Kentucky and Florida, and has been a consultant to groups seeking to utilize local history in classroom teaching.

Preface

No historian has made a greater impact upon United States history than Frederick Jackson Turner; for, from the summer evening in 1893 when Turner read his essay about the significance of the frontier to our own time, the study and teaching of American history has been conditioned by the "frontier thesis." Moreover, the efforts of historians to uphold the Turner thesis, or to attack it, have resulted in unprecedented research and reinterpretation of United States history. The end products of this effort have been a sounder understanding of America's past, the utilization of knowledge and methodology from various academic disciplines, and the realization that the study and interpretation of the past is a never-ending process.

The hypothesis which Turner presented gave a partial explanation for the uniqueness of the American character in the country's frontier experience. During the three-hundred-year process of settling the continent, there had existed not one but several frontiers, each differing somewhat from all the others. The first frontier, on the shores of the Atlantic Ocean, was unquestionably European in nature. But each succeeding line of frontier settlement lay farther in the West and was more remote from the source of European civilization, and these newer frontiers were populated largely by settlers who came, not from Europe, but from the older American settlements. Each new frontier repeated the process of settlement, but with some variations. Gradually many of the qualities of European civilization were cast aside as the settlers adapted themselves to the exigencies of frontier survival. Thus, in the ever-renewing process of settlement, the European character disappeared; and what emerged on the most westward frontier was the American character, with all its traits: unshakable faith in democracy, independence and self-sufficiency, and strong nationalism. In this process, Turner believed, was to be found the real genius of the American character.

The frontier thesis which Turner outlined did not attract immediate attention. Before long, however, the thesis fired the imagination of nearly all historians; and it produced loyal supporters and equally staunch opponents. Indeed, no other historical thesis was so widely debated in the first half of the present century; and Turner's death in 1932 in no way diminished the controversy. To elevate any single approach or interpretation to the position of being the only valid framework for understanding United States history is, of course, to invite attack. The opposition to the hypothesis that developed at about the time of Turner's death reached its climax in the 1940s. Since that time, scholarly attitude concerning the thesis has established itself between the extremes of absolute acceptance and total rejection. The attitude today recognizes Turner's contribution for what it was—a tentative hypothesis, a partial explanation for the development of the American character—but the validity of the hypothesis continues to be debated.

Turner's writing, particularly his essays on the significance of the frontier and of regional sections, precipitated an incredible amount of activity in scholarly circles. Historians and scholars from other academic disciplines have produced a staggering volume of literature bearing upon Turner's ideas; and, while the amount of such writing has diminished in recent years, it by no means has come to an end. Librarians, even now hard pressed to find shelf space for "Turner material," are well advised to prepare for additional acquisitions.

Unfortunately, much of the material written about the Turner theses, and much of Turner's own writing, appeared in somewhat obscure publications, many of them not readily available to the general reading public. Added to this difficulty is the fact that writing related to Turner's ideas has appeared over a span of years from 1893 to the present. In view of these impediments to the study of Turner's work and of his influence upon American historiography, it seems reasonable to present, in convenient, readily available form, the major ideas expressed by this preeminent American historian, together with some of the most pertinent material written about the frontier thesis.

But Professor Turner's influence upon historians and historiography transcended the impact of his writing. Turner's scholarly ability and his warm and friendly personality left an indelible mark upon students and colleagues alike. For this reason, it has been considered advisable to include in this volume something of Turner's personal life—a life devoted to intellectual curiosity and activity, to his country, and to his students and colleagues. Professor Turner's influence extended to every corner of the nation, and his sincere interest in his students continued long after the last one had graduated. His work with the American Historical Association resulted in much improvement in both the historical profession and in the teaching of history.

The attempt, then, has been to bring together in this book the major ideas which Turner expressed and some of the reaction which these ideas stimulated. An additional attempt has been made to present information about Turner the man and the teacher because this is vital in understanding his impact upon the study and teaching of United States history. However, this volume is in no way intended to be a thoroughgoing study of Turner; for the major purpose is to bring together not only the basic ideas involved in the Turner thesis, but also the points of view which that thesis stimulated, and to present these, together with pertinent information concerning Professor Turner, in a form both readily available and easily understood.

An undertaking of this nature incurs debts to many people, and the writer wishes to express his thanks to his colleagues for valuable suggestions and criticisms; to the reference and periodicals staffs of Margie Helm Library for their unfailing assistance and courtesy; to Western Kentucky University for a sabbatical semester; and to Professor Sylvia Bowman, Editor of this Series, for her patience and help. My greatest thanks go to my wife, Nina Hight Bennett, for encouragement and understanding.

JAMES D. BENNETT

Western Kentucky University

Chronology

1861   Frederick Jackson Turner born November 14 at Portage, Wisconsin. Parents: Andrew Jackson Turner (1832-1905), newspaper editor and political leader; and Mary Hanford Turner (1834-1906).

1878   Graduated from Portage High School. Awarded prize for graduation oration, "Power of the Press."

1878-   Worked as typesetter in father's newspaper office.
1880

1880   Entered University of Wisconsin. As undergraduate, began study of Wisconsin history using original materials from the Draper Collection at the State Historical Society of Wisconsin.

1884   Awarded bachelor of arts degree, University of Wisconsin.

1884-   Newspaper correspondent for Chicago and Milwaukee papers.
1885

1885-   Tutor of rhetoric and oratory, University of Wisconsin.
1888

1888   Awarded master of arts degree by University of Wisconsin; thesis on the Indian trade in Wisconsin.

1888-   Graduate student, Johns Hopkins University.
1889

1889   November 7: married Caroline Mae Sherwood in Chicago. Children: Jackson Allen Turner (1892-99); Mae Sherwood Turner (1894-99); Dorothy Kinsley Turner (Mrs. John S. Main) 1890-).

1889-   Assistant Professor of History, University of Wisconsin.
1891

1890   Awarded doctor of philosophy degree, Johns Hopkins University.

1891	Publication of doctoral dissertation, *The Character and Influence of the Indian Trade in Wisconsin.*
1891– 1892	Professor of History, University of Wisconsin.
1892– 1910	Professor of American History, University of Wisconsin.
1893	Read paper on "The Significance of the Frontier in American History" at Chicago meeting of the American Historical Association.
1896	Received but declined offer from Princeton University.
1900	Invited to head the Department of History at the University of Chicago; declined the offer.
1900– 1901	Turner, his wife, and daughter spent half year in Europe (August–February).
1904	Visiting professor at Harvard for one term.
1905	Received but declined offer from Stanford University.
1906	Publication of *The Rise of the New West, 1819–1829.*
1908	Received honorary doctor of laws and letters degree from the University of Illinois.
1908	Refuted criticism from regents of the University of Wisconsin.
1909	Received Doctor of Literature degree and offer from Harvard University; accepted offer.
1910	Began tenure at Harvard as professor of history.
1910– 1911	President, American Historical Association.
1910– 1915	Member, board of editors, *American Historical Review.*
1911	Published first edition of *List of References on History of the West.*
1912	Published *Guide to the Study and Reading of American History,* edited with Edward Channing and Albert Bushnell Hart.
1914	Summer lectures, University of Washington and University of Oregon.
1914– 1916	President, Colonial Society of Massachusetts.
1915	Lectured in summer session, University of California.
1916– 1917	Research Associate, Department of Historical Research, Carnegie Institution.

1917	Member, National Board of Historical Service; delivered Lowell Lectures, Boston, Massachusetts.
1920	Published *The Frontier in American History*.
1921	Received doctor of literature degree from the University of Wisconsin.
1922	Published "Sections and the Nation" in the *Yale Review*.
1924	Retired from Harvard; lectured in summer session at Utah State Agricultural College, Logan, Utah.
1924–1926	Lectured at the University of Wisconsin while living in Madison.
1925	Gave summer lectures, Utah State Agricultural College.
1927–1932	Research Associate, Henry E. Huntington Library, San Marino, California.
1932	March 14: died in Pasadena, California; publication of *The Significance of Sections in American History* (introduction by Max Farrand). Awarded posthumously the Pulitzer Prize.
1935	Publication of *The United States, 1830–1850: The Nation and Its Sections* (introduction by Avery Craven).
1938	Publication of *The Early Writings of Frederick Jackson Turner* (compiled by Everett E. Edwards, with an introduction by Fulmer Mood).
1966	Publication of *Frederick Jackson Turner's Legacy: Unpublished Writings in American History* (introduction by Wilbur R. Jacobs).

CHAPTER 1

Frederick Jackson Turner

FREDERICK Jackson Turner was born in Portage, Wisconsin, on November 14, 1861. His parents, Andrew Jackson and Mary Hanford Turner, were pioneer settlers in Wisconsin who had migrated from upstate New York. Portage had at that time only recently passed the frontier stage, and the town was on the edge of virtually unsettled wilderness country. Certainly young Turner's life was influenced by his growing up so near the frontier and by his daily contact with many persons who had been a part of the frontier experience.

Portage, on the banks of the Wisconsin River, is located at the beginning of a portage between that river and the Fox River. The portage was first used by Louis Jolliet and Father Marquette in 1673, and then by a succession of explorers, missionaries, and traders. Fort Winnebago was established on the portage in 1828, and an Indian Agency headquarters was erected in 1832. The town of Portage, which grew up around the headquarters, still retained much of its frontier quality when Turner was growing up there: and, for an inquisitive and impressionable boy, there were many heady reminders of the past. Turner has written that "there were still Indian tepees where I hunted and fished, and Indians came into the stores to buy paints and trinkets and to sell furs."[1] Indians, dogs, and ponies, he said, were familiar sights on the streets of Portage.

Acquisition of statehood by Wisconsin in 1848 coincided with the great migration of Germans to the United States, many of whom settled in the new state. Portage's strategic location on the portage between the Wisconsin and Fox rivers placed it squarely across a major path of the westward movement. People of diverse national origins passed through the area, and some of them settled to form the nucleus of a frontier village that developed around the fort. Turner recalled that the population of Portage in his youth included

Irish, Pomeranians, Scotch, Welsh, Germans, New England Yankees, New York Yankees, a few Southerners, a few Negroes, some
Englishmen, one or two Italians, and many Norwegians and Swiss.[2]
It was truly a melting pot on the frontier, and the fact that they all
"got on together" was a tribute to the working of frontier democracy.

Turner watched the raftsmen floating logs down the river from
the pine forests of northern Wisconsin, and he talked with men
recently returned from the mines of Colorado and the ranches of
Montana. He rode on the first railroad into the pine forests; he
fished rivers and lakes whose French names recalled the early
explorers of the region; and he followed Indian trails on hunting
expeditions. For the youthful Turner, there was no escaping the
past; the frontier experience surrounded him. The town of Portage,
in the 1860s and 1870s, was in a transitional period; and residents
could see the successive waves of settlement which changed the
area from a land sparsely dotted with Indian tepees to one in which
large-scale agriculture and the beginnings of industrialization were
dominant.

Turner was a part of all this change, and his position in the community provided him with an ideal vantage point for observing the
process of settlement and development. The elder Turner was
editor of the local newspaper, an avid local historian, and a leader in
the area's political activities. Working in the newspaper office,
young Turner must have been well informed about local happen-
ings, must have known of the growing problems of the farmers, and
must have learned a great deal about how party politics worked at
the grass roots level. Few young men have had such an ideal opportunity not only to witness the development of a region from raw
frontier to cosmopolitan community but to participate to such a
great extent in the process of democratic living.

In the small town of Portage, then, Fred Turner could see the
world in microcosm; a veritable parade of nationalities filled the
streets, proclaiming the traits and characteristics of a dozen nations.
But, with the passing of time, the careful observer could note that
nationalistic distinctions became less noticeable and could actually
see the development of a new national character that recalled European origins, of course, but that exhibited many differences unique
to the time and place. Turner was witnessing the very process of
American development in his hometown. Here, also, as Carl Becker

has noted, "past and present curiously joined together; the frontier in many stages—virgin forest, Indian villages, lawless raftsmen, fur trade, the rough frontier town" combined to form a new society.[3] What Turner saw stayed with him for the rest of his life and provided him with a framework for understanding American history.

I *The Significant Years of Turner's Youth*

If fate determined a particularly appropriate place for the future historian of the frontier to spend his youth, that same fate exercised as much discretion in choosing the time. What we may refer to as Turner's formative period, that time from his birth in 1861 to the July day in 1893 when he read his now famous essay on "The Significance of the Frontier in American History," coincided with what Robert G. Albion has termed the era of the "Communications Revolution."[4] These thirty-two years witnessed "a series of remarkable developments which rightly may be judged as unprecedented in all history."[5] This period, so often referred to as the Industrial Revolution, produced virtually unprecedented changes in all phases of American life—changes which were particularly significant for the future of the agrarian West.

Of all the aspects of the industrial and communications revolutions, none had more influence upon the agriculture of the American West than did the Civil War and the westward expansion of the railroad. War generates an almost insatiable appetite for all manner of agricultural products; and, so long as fighting continues, there is no appreciable reduction in the demand for these goods. With the outbreak of hostilities in 1861, American farmers were called upon to produce greater quantities of goods than had ever been needed in the past, and to produce them with a war-drained labor supply. That they were able successfully to meet this challenge was due in large measure to the fact that there existed in the United States a surprising number and variety of agricultural implements which substantially reduced the amount of labor necessary to produce a given quantity of goods. For the most part, these implements had been available since the first half of the nineteenth century; but they had been little used because of their high cost; they were expensive, also, because a sufficient supply of farm labor was available, thereby eliminating the necessity of supplementing human labor with machines in order to meet the fairly modest demands of the domestic market. The call to arms, which was eventually answered by hundreds of thousands of young men, thus broke through this stalemated situation; with an increased demand and a decreased labor market, agricultural machinery was essential. It also appeared essential that the vast acreage of the trans-Mississippi West be opened to cultivation, and the railroad proved to be the key which unlocked the agricultural resources of the West.

Few examples of the communications revolution are more spectacular than the growth of American railroads. Between 1870 and 1890, 110,000 miles of railroad lines were constructed, a large proportion of that construction occurring in the West. These roads provided a comparatively easy and rapid means of carrying settlers into previously unsettled areas, thus accelerating the process of settlement and opening vast expanses of land to agricultural production. At the same time, these railroads, each year penetrating more deeply into unoccupied lands, were the means of carrying goods to markets. Coupled with the developments in shipping, the communications improvements that resulted from the Atlantic cable and the telephone, the greater efficiency that resulted from business consolidation, and the opening of the Suez Canal in 1869, the railroads were soon a vital link connecting the Western farmer with markets all over the world.

This technological growth, so important to the United States during the Civil War, was not an unmixed blessing to the farmer who had rushed into the West and begun to cultivate the land he had homesteaded; for it was soon apparent that the United States was not the only nation which was experiencing an expansion of its agricultural output. The forces which had made possible agricultural growth in the western United States also opened up vast acreages in Australia, Argentina, and Canada. The American farmer, before the end of the nineteenth century, was competing with many others on an international market. Moreover, despite a slight increase in world per capita consumption of agricultural goods, technological innovations were constantly increasing the productivity of American lands and of American farm labor.

As a result of the industrial and communications revolutions, with their new farm machinery, their thousands of miles of railroad lines, and their rapid communication, the agricultural potential of millions of acres of land was exploited. The resulting vast supply of agricultural goods inundated even the growing world market, thereby producing, inevitably, a decline in the price of agricultural commodities. The farmer became the victim of his own success.

This economic distress resulted in discontentment among farmers in many parts of the world and was experienced by American farmers most acutely in the last decade of the century.[6] Increasingly, American farmers turned to politics in their search for a means of alleviating their distress. Belatedly they realized that their world, and their position in it, had changed. Thomas Jefferson's independent farmer was no longer the prime mover and decision-maker in the United States. In the age of industry, the industrialist and the financier charted the direction the nation would follow; agriculture's showing in the election of 1896 was a fair indication of the role it would play in the future. Frederick Jackson Turner saw and experienced this shift in power and production from his special vantage point in the newspaper office of a small town on the recent frontier.

II *Turner's Education at the State University*

Important as Turner's environment and his times were in shaping his philosophy and understanding of his country, his ideas were perhaps crystallized by the education he received at the state university. Turner has offered no explanation as to why he chose to enter the University of Wisconsin, but it was located close by in the adjoining county, and, perhaps, as was the case with Carl Becker, who was later a student of Turner's, he knew someone who had "been at Madison."[7] For whatever reasons, his choice of the university was, as Merle Curti has noted, "an all-important step in Turner's development. . . ."[8] The University of Wisconsin in 1880 was, when Turner began his freshman semester two years after his graduation from Portage High School, a relatively small and highly democratic school. Its president, John Bascom, was a progressive leader, who had advanced ideas about social and economic issues. Bascom believed that university students, whose education was provided for largely by the state, had an obligation to the people of the state; he urged university graduates to use their education for the improvement of the state and of its people. This philosophy was further developed under the leadership of President Thomas C. Chamberlin, and it resulted in an extensive and effective statewide program of extension courses offered by the university that were designed to take education to citizens who could not attend classes on the campus and to improve the quality of life of the taxpayers who supported the activities of the university. Chamberlin

suggested that history should be included in the extension offerings
and later Turner, as a young and energetic member of the history
department, was involved in this activity. The extension work of the
university squared well with Turner's democratic concepts and this
work provided him for many years with a forum before which he
developed his ideas.

At the university, Turner acquired a sound classical education.
His own later writing, characterized by a "sensitiveness to literary
style. . . fluid and balanced sentences," and a "liking for the apt
epithet, owed something to his classical studies."[9] More important-
ly, however, the small size of the university permitted a close community association with professors and students alike and must have
strengthened in Turner the democratic tendencies which had been
nurtured during his formative years in Portage. His belief in a
democratic society was stated convincingly in two prize-winning
orations, one given during his junior year at the university; the
other, at his commencement exercises in 1884.[10]

During these years as an undergraduate at the University of Wisconsin, Turner came into contact with two forces which were to
change the course of his life. One of these was the Draper Collection housed in the library of the State Historical Society of Wisconsin. This magnificent collection of manuscripts had been assembled
by Lyman C. Draper, a founder of the State Historical Society of
Wisconsin, over a period of fifty years. Rather surprisingly, the
young undergraduate was "given the freedom of the Draper Collection . . . and the friendship of Draper. . . . "[11] Reading in these
manuscripts provided Turner with both the ideas and the sources
for his first article, "History of the 'Grignon Tract' on the Portage of
the Fox and Wisconsin Rivers."[12] Moreover, he found extensive
material about the fur trade, the subject which he later chose for his
doctoral dissertation. The manuscripts in the Draper Collection
were one of the two forces which, he said, caused him to see
"American history somewhat differently than it was presented in the
books I read."[13]

The other force in establishing the direction of his professional
life, and the more important one by far, was his association with
William F. Allen, a professor of history at Wisconsin. Turner was
introduced to American history when he took Allen's course during
his junior year; such was the impact of the man that Turner, when

he returned to the university as a graduate student and as an instructor in rhetoric and oratory, enrolled in Allen's "seminary," as a seminar was then known, and declared his intention of securing the master of arts degree in history. By all accounts Professor Allen was a highly effective and stimulating teacher. After receiving the master of arts degree from Harvard, Allen had studied in Göttingen, where he had fallen under the spell of Arnold H. L. Heeren, and then in Berlin and in Rome. His study in Germany, in the 1850s, coincided with the great development of scholarship and historical method which brought fame to the German universities. Allen was widely traveled, in both Europe and the United States; he was trained in the newest methods of historical research and instruction; and he was that rare academic figure, the general historian. While his great interest was in Roman history, his breadth and depth of knowledge enabled him to do research and to offer outstanding courses in European and American history. As a result of this training, Allen introduced methods of research and teaching which were novel in the United States at the time.

Professor Allen's method differed from that employed by most university history professors at the time in two highly significant ways. First of all, Allen was an exponent of the "scientific approach" to the study of history; he stressed the importance of the critical evaluation of primary sources in any attempt to understand and explain the past. In the use of this "scientific method," Allen reflected the current trend in German scholarship and was one of the first successful practitioners of the method in the United States. This approach, which demanded access to primary resources, worked particularly well at Wisconsin, because students in the Department of History were permitted to use the Draper Collection of the State Historical Society.

Second, Allen esmphasized the economic and cultural aspects of history at a time when most American history professors concentrated on constitutional and political implications. The highly controversial doctrine of evolution was used by Allen to show the gradual, but uninterrupted development of society, to point out the evolutionary nature of civilization. And, while most teachers urged the mastery of bare facts in textbooks, Allen taught the complex interrelationships between Europe and the United States. Turner studied his professor as well as his sources; and, when he himself began teaching, much of Allen's method and style became Turner's own.

Other techniques developed and used by Professor Allen were employed later by Turner, techniques which help to explain his remarkable ability as a teacher. Allen was fond of using maps, particularly in explaining the expansion of Roman civilization across Europe, and in showing the movements of peoples.[14] It is not surprising, then, that Turner throughout his career spent much time studying maps, census reports, and statistics recording the movements of people across the United States. Allen's practice was to employ topical organization in his courses and to prepare syllabi and reading lists for his classes, practices later used extensively by Turner.

Professor Allen's influence upon Turner was not confined to the classroom. The teacher and his student became close personal friends, Turner being an almost daily visitor in Allen's home. It seems to have been a mutually rewarding relationship; the older man enjoyed the companionship of this vigorous young man with his inquisitive and highly developed mind; and Turner profited from mature and original insights into the study and teaching of history offered by Allen. Perhaps, as Fulmer Mood has suggested, Allen saw in Turner the future fulfillment of his own dreams and aspirations; and he may have regarded the training of Turner as his greatest contribution to the historical profession.[15] Turner, for his part, never forgot the benefits he had derived from association with this remarkable man; and he once expressed his debt to his old professor by saying that "Allen taught me all the history I know."[16]

After Turner graduated from the University of Wisconsin in 1884, he spent the following year as a reporter on a Madison newspaper. But his love of history and his academic experiences as an undergraduate proved to be strong influences upon Turner, and he returned in the following year to the campus to prepare himself for a university teaching career. Turner received an appointment as tutor in oratory and rhetoric in the university, and embarked upon coursework for the master of arts degree in history. During his second year of graduate work, Turner began teaching in the Department of History; and in the following year his instructional assignment shifted primarily to that field, although he continued to have some duties in oratory and rhetoric. The university catalog description of

Turner's first course offering indicates the influence of Professor Allen: "American history . . . Allen's History Topics with any good U.S. History of the higher grade; Johnston, Leeds and Higginson's Larger History are especially recommended. Outline maps are used for marking territorial changes."[17] The use of maps, and the process of studying history by topics, which would figure so prominently in his later seminars, were features of his courses from the beginning.

Turner was awarded the master of arts degree in 1888. As one of the requirements for the degree, Turner presented a thesis entitled "The Influence of the Fur Trade in the Development of Wisconsin."[18] The central theme of this thesis, the history of the fur trade in Wisconsin, had interested Turner since his first course with Professor Allen in his junior year. As part of the work for that course Turner had written an essay which touched on the early history of the fur trade.[19] Turner's interest in the fur trade continued and this theme, in expanded form, was the subject of his doctoral dissertation at Johns Hopkins University.

By the time Turner received the master of arts degree, he was engaged in almost all the routine activities of a full-time faculty member. The number of students in the Department of History was increasing, and Turner was offering an advanced course in American history. He had published one article, on the Grignon tract; had written a book review; and, in 1888, had produced his *Outline Studies in the History of the Northwest*. These publications represented a not inconsiderable output for a part-time teacher who was still working on the master's degree. Moreover, there was every indication that he was rapidly establishing himself as an effective and stimulating teacher.

Turner, of course, was not unaware of the professional development he had achieved; and, perhaps on the strength of this, he applied to President Chamberlin for an increase in salary for the coming academic year. When Chamberlin's reply was not favorable, Turner decided to pursue the doctoral degree at Johns Hopkins. It can hardly be assumed that Chamberlin was dissatisfied with Turner's work, or that he sought to discourage the young scholar; on the contrary, it may be, as Mood has suggested, that Chamberlin sought to convince Turner of the advisability of obtaining the advanced degree.[20] Indeed, such an objective on Chamberlin's part is

suggested by the fact that Turner's name was not dropped from the
university's course listings during his absence and that Turner listed
additional courses he planned to teach when he returned.

III   Turner at Johns Hopkins

Turner entered the Johns Hopkins University at the beginning of
the 1888–89 school year. This proved to be a rich and rewarding
year for Turner. He took a broad selection of courses—church history, history of politics, economic principles, international law—
under some of the most stimulating and scholarly professors the
nation provided.[21] These instructors included Albion Small, the
sociologist; Richard T. Ely, who stressed the historical approach to
the study of economics; and Woodrow Wilson, whose *Congressional
Government* had quickened Turner's interest in the question of
American nationality. His dissertation was to be under the supervi-
sion of Herbert Baxter Adams, the most widely known university
professor in the United States at the time. All these men exerted an
influence upon Turner, and he formed lifelong friendships with
some of them. He also had the association of some of the brightest
and most conscientious students in the country; for Johns Hopkins,
which was already developing a reputation as the outstanding
graduate school in the country, drew students from every section of
the nation.[22]

In his studies with Adams, Turner was exposed to the "germ
concept" of historical development, which held that modern American society had evolved from earlier European political forms, such
as the "folk moot," which had been traced to Teutonic tribes that
once inhabited the forests of Germany. Allen also had stressed the
evolutionary approach to the development of current civilization,
but Adams emphasized the superiority of heredity over environment to a far greater extent than Allen had done. Although Turner
was not able to accept Adam's emphasis, he could agree that heredity might explain the similarities between Europe and the United
States: but he felt that the many differences between the two areas
could be explained only by environment. The experiences of his
youth and his study of the Wisconsin fur trade had indicated to him
the influence which physical surroundings had upon the shaping of
society and institutions, and he was doubtless also affected by the
rising wave of sectional awareness and pride, which was developing
in the West. He and Wilson—who, as a visiting lecturer at Johns

Hopkins, was staying at the same boarding house where Turner and another bright young student, Charles H. Haskins, lived—engaged in more than one discussion about the undue prominence usually given to New England in the development of the United States and about the need to show the prominent role which had been played by the South and the West.[23]

Despite the divergent philosophies of Turner and Adams concerning the development of American civilization, they got along together well; and Turner was soon engaged in preparing his dissertation. He wanted to use the fur trade in Wisconsin for his subject, thereby precluding the need for "starting from scratch" with a new research topic; and, when Adams agreed to this proposal, he suggested various changes and reorganization. In its final form, the dissertation, "The Character and Influence of the Indian Trade in Wisconsin: A Study of the Trading Post as an Institution," fitted the style of institutional history which was then the fashion at Johns Hopkins. Perhaps because Turner knew that Adams doubted that the West had any institutions worthy of serious study, he was careful to trace the history of the trading post to Phoenician and Roman times, thereby providing it with a history far older than that of the German folk moots and at the same time giving a western institution sufficient historical and academic "respectability" to satisfy even the fastidious Adams. The dissertation was completed after Turner returned to Madison, and he received his doctorate in 1890.[24]

Turner benefited in many ways from his year at Baltimore. He studied under outstanding teachers, and he associated with brilliant young students who, like himself, later fulfilled their early bright promise. Moreover, he formed lasting friendships with many of these associates. Turner was largely responsible for bringing Professor Ely to the Madison campus, and he was able to lure Haskins from the East to a position as the other professor in Wisconsin's history department shortly after the death of Allen. He maintained contact with Adams and shared his interest in the development of education, catching much of Adams's excitement in the Chatauqua movement and incorporating it later in his own work with university extension. Turner and Wilson remained warm friends over the years, each frequently seeking the advice of the other about their various projects.

But Turner had remained in close touch with Allen and with university affairs at Madison during his absence. He was a keen student of teaching methods; and, in frequent letters to Allen, he reported his observations, made comparisons between methods used at Wisconsin and at Johns Hopkins, and suggested courses he would like to develop upon his return to the Wisconsin campus.[25] When Turner returned to Madison for the fall term of 1889, he did not yet have his degree: but, since his dissertation was well in hand, he was looking forward to active, full-time teaching and research and to renewing his association with Professor Allen.

IV *Assistant Professor at Wisconsin*

There seems to have been, as we have suggested, at least a tacit understanding that Turner would return to the University of Wisconsin following his year of study at Johns Hopkins. He maintained an active correspondence with Professor Allen, who kept him apprised of activities in the history department; and the class schedule for the academic year 1889–90, which was developed in the spring of 1889, indicated a full schedule of courses to be taught by Turner. Turner's teaching load consisted of four courses. He resumed the teaching of an elementary course in United States history, and he again offered work in the history of the Northwest. In addition, he was scheduled to offer a course on the history of nineteenth-century Europe, and an advanced lecture course on American constitutional and political history—a course which reflected Turner's work at Johns Hopkins.

This course indicates, also, that Turner had not forgotten the talks he had had with Woodrow Wilson concerning western and southern sectionalism and the idea of American patriotism. The catalog description indicated that the course would be studied from original sources, with additional readings from standard histories, and that an entire college year would be devoted to the course. Special emphasis would be given to the growth of American nationality and to the development of the Constitution by interpretation and usage. The fact that the course would pay particular attention to the rise of state and local institutions reflects the influence of Herbert Baxter Adams. Turner devoted most of his attention to this course, and it provided him with opportunity to develop additionally his ideas concerning the uniqueness of American nationality.[26]

All other work in the department was handled by Professor Allen; these two men constituted the Department of History of the University of Wisconsin. Reunited on the Madison campus, involved in the affairs of a growing university, and conducting the course work of a history department whose reputation was growing steadily, these two friends viewed their work as a labor of love and anticipated a long and pleasant association. But such happy hopes were not to be realized.

V *Death of Professor Allen*

Professor Allen was, in December, 1889, correcting and revising proofs of his book, *A Short History of the Roman People*. He had just completed this work and had announced that the manuscript was ready for publication when he died on December 9. Allen's death was a profound shock to Turner. Writing to Herbert Adams at the request of Mrs. Allen, Turner confided that "I can hardly bear to write the words" of his death, "nor can I make them seem true."[27] Although Allen had been ill with a severe cold which had kept him from campus, his physicians had reported improvement; and, on the strength of that report, Turner and his wife had left Madison for Portage where they were to attend a reception. Upon his return from Portage on Sunday evening, he had met a group of professors as he left the Madison depot and had been informed of Allen's death. "I have been stunned ever since," he said. His sense of loss was admirably stated in the concluding lines of his letter to Adams: "And so the gentlest, justest, most scholarly man I ever knew, has gone."[28]

Turner's painful adjustment to the loss of his friend was rendered more difficult by the situation in the Department of History caused by Allen's death. The most immediate problem, of course, was that of making arrangements for continuing Allen's classes; but of even greater importance in the long run was the matter of choosing a new department head. An interim arrangement was effected whereby Turner taught the courses which had been offered by Allen, and an assistant was brought in to conduct Turner's classes. This arrangement was a temporary expedient, however; the assistant's engagement was for one year only, and President Chamberlin gave indication that he was considering Turner as Allen's successor.

As a matter of fact, the past relationship between Turner and the university president had offered nothing to indicate that Turner would be considered for the position of chairman. Turner has written that when he returned to the university in 1889, Chamberlin had been reluctant to "make any tangible arrangement with me";

and he had done so only after a great deal of prodding from Allen
and after Turner had announced that he would wait no longer for a
decision. Thus, Turner had been left dangling about the job, "left to
await the spring market," he said, a situation which he had found
less than pleasing. As frustrating as such a position had been it had
been all the more difficult because "President Chamberlin's actions
will be entirely impossible of prediction, and in meantime I am kept
like Mohammed's coffin."[29]

But others shared Turner's concern for his future, and interest in
the development in the Wisconsin history department was not limited to the Madison campus. Woodrow Wilson was one of those who
kept an alert eye upon developments, or the lack of them, at Wisconsin, and from his home in Connecticut he sought some way in
which he could turn the balance in favor of Turner. It was difficult,
even awkward, for Wilson to intervene on Turner's behalf because
Wilson knew neither President Chamberlin nor anyone at the university who could serve as an intermediary—and Chamberlin certainly had not asked Wilson for his opinion. Wilson's interest in
advancing Turner for the position soon overcame these obstacles,
however, and the future president of the United States, in his forth-
right way, wrote Chamberlin on behalf of Turner. In a letter to
Reuben Gold Thwaites, Wilson indicated the tack he had taken with
Chamberlin: "I take it for granted that there is practically no doubt
about his succeeding Professor Allen, by whom he was much ad-
mired and whose natural successor he would seem to be." Wilson
also stated that he was sure that he was writing "in the interests of
historical scholarship in America in thus insisting upon being allowed to speak in his [Turner's] praise."[30]

President Chamberlin was unquestionably influenced by Wilson's action and by this eastern professor's praise of Turner.
Nevertheless, the president took no precipitate action. About a
week after Allen's death Chamberlin asked Turner who would make
a good successor to Allen, and he mentioned the names of some
men he evidently had in mind for the position. Turner did not know
these people, and he suggested in reply to the question that either
Woodrow Wilson or Ephraim Emerton of Harvard would fully
satisfy his own requirements for a department head. Chamberlin
gave no indication that Turner was among those whom he was considering to succeed Allen.[31] Thus matters stood until the following

year. In the meantime, Turner took his examinations in history, political science, and international law, and won his doctoral degree from Johns Hopkins.[32]

In 1890, President Chamberlin acted to place Turner in Allen's old chair; and to help him he called the precocious Charles Haskins from an instructorship in European history at Johns Hopkins to a similar position at Madison. Thus, at the beginning of the 1890–91 academic year, the Department of History of the University of Wisconsin was in the hands of two "Hopkins men" who bore the stamp of approval of the renowned Professor Adams and of Woodrow Wilson, and for whom great promise already had been predicted. President Chamberlin, so anxious to improve the quality of his faculty and to raise the level of teaching and research at his university, had indeed made a wise selection. In the fall, Turner—only twenty-nine, head of a university history department, and soon to be named to the rank of full professor—and Haskins—twenty years of age, and to become a professor in three years—began to work together to develop historical activity at the university.[33]

Turner was soon involved in a variety of activities. At the request of Mrs. Allen, Turner assumed the role of literary executor for his old friend; and he wrote an admiring and perceptive preface to Allen's *A Short History of the Roman People.* In addition to supervising the affairs of the department and carrying a heavy teaching assignment, Turner found time occasionally to write book reviews, supervise the work of his first graduate students, and make continuous revision of his own courses. Moreover, he was soon devoting a considerable amount of time and energy to a new university program.

VI *The University Extension Program*

President Chamberlin was now ready to launch his new university-extension program whereby he hoped to share with citizens of Wisconsin some of the benefits to be derived from the tax-supported state university. He envisioned a series of lecture courses which would enrich the social and cultural experiences of those residents who could not themselves go to the Madison campus. Chamberlin must have seen in the university-extension movement an opportunity to make the university a vital, positive force for the improvement of life and for the development of good citizenship, as well as a chance to prove the value of the university to taxpayers across the state. He asked Turner and other leading members of the faculty to participate in the undertaking.

Turner willingly lent his support to the extension program, for he doubtless found in it many similarities to the Chatauqua program which had been successfully launched several years earlier in the East and which Herbert Adams had enthusiastically supported. Chamberlin felt that history was a proper subject to be included in the courses for extension study, and Turner agreed to prepare a course. In the fall of 1891 his essay "The Significance of History" appeared in two successive numbers of the *Wisconsin Journal of Education.*[34] In this essay Turner attempted to accomplish several things; to define history (the self-consciousness of humanity), to state its utility (it affords a training ground for good citizenship), and to give practical instruction to teachers (use all the resources available to make history live). "The school-teacher," Turner stated, "is called to do a work above and beyond the instruction in his school. He is called upon to be the apostle of the higher culture to the community in which he is placed."[35]

In the same year, he produced a syllabus for a course of six lectures on the colonization of North America for use in the university-extension program;[36] and, in the following year, he wrote an article on Wisconsin's extension program for *University Extension: A Monthly Journal Devoted to the Interests of Popular Education.*[37] But these essays were not the extent of Turner's involvement in the extension program: he traveled the length and breadth of the state delivering a heavy schedule of lectures, an undertaking he continued until he was convinced that the extension program no longer provided him a suitable teaching situation.

Turner was particularly successful in his lectures on various college campuses throughout the state; however, despite his outstanding ability as a public speaker, less scholarly audiences found his lectures somewhat deep for pleasant listening or easy comprehension. Joseph Schafer, in a review of *The Early Writings of Frederick Jackson Turner* printed in the *Wisconsin Magazine of History*, quotes the director of the extension program as saying that Turner ". . . was not a success as an extension lecturer." The same source gives Turner's explanation for abandoning his extension lectures: "I gave up extension lecturing because I found I could not tell the truth."[38]

VII *Turner's First Advanced Students*

Turner's teaching did not suffer from the attention which he had devoted to his duties as department head and to the development of the extension program. The word spread that Turner's courses were lively and intellectually stimulating, and his classes were soon attracting a growing number of students. In his first year after his return from Johns Hopkins, he began training his first graduate students; and through their work much can be seen of Turner's own interests, ideas, and methods. Therefore, it is particularly revealing to look at the topics on which some of these students were working.

Turner's first graduate student was Emory Richard Johnson. As an undergraduate at Madison, he had taken courses with both Allen and Turner, had enjoyed them immensely, and had proved to be a good student—good enough to try for honors in history at graduation. At Turner's suggestion, Johnson wrote an essay on internal improvements from 1822 to 1840 for his honors work.[39] The following year, Johnson enrolled at Johns Hopkins where he wrote a paper on river and harbor bills for Herbert Adams. He returned to Wisconsin in the fall of 1890 and completed his master of arts degree in 1891 under Turner's direction. In the same year, Johnson read his thesis, "River and Harbor Bills," before a meeting of the American Academy of Political and Social Sciences at Philadelphia.[40] There followed two years of work at the University of Pennsylvania, which in 1893 awarded him his doctorate. His thesis on inland waterways as a means of transportation was a continuation of the subject which Turner had suggested for his honors essay.

Other able students followed Johnson through Turner's seminar; and, like him, many of them went on to complete theses or dissertations under Turner's direction. In most cases their subjects reflected Turner's concern with the development of the country—the continuous move of population westward and the subjugation of the wilderness; the origins and methods of this movement; and, finally, the emergence of a unique culture in the recently settled area. To that end, Albert Hart Sanford studied schemes to secure federal aid for internal improvements in Wisconsin; Miss Kate Everest did outstanding work in the area of immigration, particularly German immigration, into Wisconsin; and Orin G. Libby introduced the concept of historical analysis in his study of *The Geographical Distribution of the Vote of the Thirteen States on the Federal Constitution, 1787–88*—a dissertation which Charles A.

Beard has called "the most important single contribution to the interpretation of the movement for the federal Constitution."[41]

A host of students moved through the seminar, well trained in the use of original sources, accustomed to giving thoughtful analysis to research material, and virtually indefatigable in their historical work. Turner was rapidly making a name for himself, and the fame of his seminar was spreading. His students were now welcome in graduate schools and to the faculties of colleges and universities in all parts of the country.

VIII *Turner's Growing Reputation*

Clearly Turner had become a personage to reckon with in the halls of academe, and it was reasonable to imagine that Turner the historian would have a strong voice in determining the direction which historical research and writing would take in the next few years. Perhaps with such thoughts in mind, Turner published in 1892 in the university newspaper an essay entitled "Problems in American History," stating his position and his interests. Appearing as it did in the undergraduate newspaper, it must also have served as an enticing advertisement for the wares offered in the Department of History. A fuller statement of Turner's concept of history was due, and it soon appeared; it was presented, however, before a larger and more critical forum, and its thesis reshaped the course of American historiography.

CHAPTER 2

The Frontier Thesis

F REDERICK Jackson Turner's statement of the frontier thesis, which later attracted the attention of almost all American and of many European historians, elicited little notice when it was first presented to the world on July 12, 1893, at an evening meeting in Chicago of a World's Congress of Historians that was held in conjunction with the World's Columbian Exposition, a gigantic, although belated, commemoration of Columbus's voyage to the New World. Here, on the shores of Lake Michigan, the shining temporary city of the fair had been constructed to serve as a showcase for America's marvelous development. Virtually endless exhibits attested to the country's material and technical growth, and visitors from all parts of the globe were properly impressed by the displays, by the architecture, and particularly by the giant Corliss dynamo which provided electrical power to light the exposition grounds. But it was not sufficient to exhibit only mechanical and material growth; the occasion required that at least passing attention should be given to intellectual and cultural development.

To that end the conference of world historians had been arranged with the assistance of the American Historical Association, and Professor Charles Kenton Adams, president of the University of Wisconsin, had invited his young head of the History Department to present a paper at that meeting.

I Immediate Reaction to the Thesis

"The Significance of the Frontier in American History," the title of the paper which Turner read that evening, announced in bold terms the hypothesis which became the foundation of the frontier thesis and which elevated its author to a position of preeminence among American historians. Rather surprisingly to later generations of scholars, for whom the "Turner thesis" was a major topic of discussion, the paper occasioned almost no comment at all. The official account of the meeting, carried in the *Independent*, made no mention of the paper; and a lengthier article chronicling the session in *Dial* magazine contained no reference to it. In fact, only one local newspaper found space—on an inside page—for even a brief reference to it. Even Turner's parents, who were visiting the exposition at the time, were not among those in attendance.[1]

The most surprising comment, perhaps, was made in the *Dial*, which noted that "amateur historians and sensational theorists had no place on the program."[2] Later historians, who regarded the thesis as a revolutionary and emancipating pronouncement, could regard this statement only as an indication that Turner's message scarcely had been understood. The response from other historians, to whom Turner sent copies of the paper, generally showed little more than polite interest. Theodore Roosevelt who, as the author of *The Winning of the West*, might have been expected to see some of the real significance of the paper, wrote Turner that the essay "struck some first class ideas, and put into definite shape a good deal of thought which has been floating around rather loosely." Edward Everett Hale thanked Turner for what he referred to rather cryptically as a "curious and interesting paper." The reply of Dr. Francis A. Walker, president of the Massachusetts Institute of Technology, who stated that "the mere title is a success in itself," would have been more encouraging had he not added that he hoped to find time in the future to read the paper. The single encouraging statement about the thesis came from Talcott Williams, an outstanding Philadelphia journalist. The paper was, declared Williams, "the most informative and illuminating contribution to American history that I have read in several years."[3]

That Turner's statement of the significance of the frontier failed to create any immediate excitement, that Williams was virtually alone in finding it "informative and illuminating," and that it was not thought to be the work of a "sensational theorist," all stemmed from the fact that it was not yet understood. Turner had to devote considerable time in the future to writing essays to explain and to expand the ideas and concepts contained in his Chicago paper; and the popularizing of the thesis and its elevation to the position of "the" explanation of American history were to be the work of a host of Turner-trained historians. So much was suggested, so much was implied in the thesis, and so much additional work to be done was outlined in it that it is small wonder that the thesis did not catch on immediately.

Of even more importance to the clear understanding of the frontier thesis is the necessity of knowing the thought processes which had led to it. Two of Turner's earlier essays, "The Significance of History," which had appeared in 1891, and "Problems in American History," which had been published in 1892, are logical antecedents to the 1893 essay. These earlier writings must be read and understood before we can approach the frontier thesis with any hope of really understanding it.

II *The Significance of History*

"The Significance of History", the first of Turner's major essays, was written at the request of President Chamberlin to call attention to the university-extension program, which was in process of being launched;[4] but the essay is remarkable for a number of reasons. In the first place, it provided a veritable catalog of the concepts of history. Turner began his essay by noting that these concepts have been almost as numerous as the men who had written history; and he then touches briefly upon some of the major ones. To some, history is literature; the skilled writer waves a magic wand over the bare bones of the past and a forgotten era springs to life, properly peopled with officers and artisans, with warriors doing battle before ruined towers miraculously restored—"the whole busy life of generations that have long ago gone down to dust comes to life again in the pages of a book." Turner cautioned against these "romantic literary artists" who did not hesitate to "paint a character blacker or whiter than he really is" in order to create more interesting literature.[5]

To other historians, Turner asserted, history was a study of politics—politics as Aristotle used the term—that embodied "all that concerns the activity of the state itself." He quoted Edward A. Freeman's statement that "history is past politics and politics present history," a statement which Professor Adams had caused to be printed on a wall of his seminar room. Turner surveyed the findings of historians who wrote from this viewpoint, from Wilhelm Maurenbrecher of Leipzig to William Stubbs.

But it was yet another school of historians, those "to whom history is the study of the economic growth of the people, the distribution of wealth, the social conditions of the people," to whom Turner was attracted. "Viewed from this position," Turner said, "the past is filled with new meaning." Economic history focuses upon the mass of people, it includes not only the "brilliant annals of the few," but the tragedy of the tiller of the soil, the slave whose labor built the "glory that was Greece," and "the serfdom into which decayed the 'grandeur that was Rome.' "

History had still different meanings to other historians. For Thomas Carlyle, the hero-worshipper, history was a stage on which a few great men acted out their parts; to Max Müller, history was found in the growth of religious ideas; to the "medieval historian, history was the annals of the monastery, or the chronicle of court and camp." Finally, in the nineteenth century, another school of historians appeared whose aim was to unite the critical study of historical materials that had survived from the past with the interpretative skill of the political expert to arrive at a better understanding of the past. Leopold von Ranke, the great German historian, applied this critical method to the study of history. Ranke's objective was, as Turner pointed out, to "tell things as they really were." It was Ranke's critical method of studying history, to which a number of American scholars were exposed in the German universities, which set the tone of historical research and writing in the United States.

As for what is to be learned from this brief cataloging of historical concepts, Turner stressed that history had to be reinterpreted for and by each generation. "Each age," Turner emphatically asserted, "writes the history of the past anew with reference to the conditions uppermost in its own time." This reinterpretation does not mean that the events of the past change, of course, but that man's comprehension of these events changes and expands in the light of his own knowledge and surroundings. Moreover, the concepts of history reflect the values and concerns dominant when the history is written: a Romantic age produced Romantic history; the scientific age which developed in the nineteenth century produced the scientific method in the writing of history.

If we accept the argument that each age must rewrite the history of the past in the light of current conditions, the value and the utility of history are the achievement of a better understanding of the past.

The better understanding of the past is in itself ample reward for our work; but, Turner maintained, because history is ever becoming, never completed, the study of the past is relevant for every age. "Today is so much a product of yesterday," Turner said, "that yesterday can only be understood as it is explained today." By the same token, we can begin to understand today only when we know the elements of the past that have been introduced into the present: "The present is simply the developing past, the past the undeveloped present." The goal of the historian is, therefore, to show the living present by revealing its origin from the past. That the past lives in the present could be demonstrated easily enough, Turner maintained: "When the inaugural procession passes toward the senate chamber, and the president's address outlines the policy he proposes to pursue, there is Rome"; and the past in the present can be seen in the legal code of Louisiana and also in the ceremonials of the Roman Catholic Church. With the broad and poetic imagery of a moving procession, which he was fond of using, Turner thus traced the process of history.

To Turner, history, the continual study of the past, was valuable, therefore, as a means of understanding the present. Historical study was valuable also for the mental growth which results from such a study: it enables a man to see his "own time and place as a part of the stupendous progress of the ages;" and it "enables us to realize the richness of our inheritance, the possibility of our lives, the grandeur of the present. . . ." But, to the practical and democratic Turner, one other value was to be derived from the study of history—it is a preeminent training ground for good citizenship; and good citizenship is doubtless the reason for the existence of the public schools. A knowledge gained through study of the history of America's past, of its interrelationship with other nations and peoples, and of the growth of its institutions is the soundest preparation for good citizenship. "Historical study has for its end to let the community see itself in the light of the past, to give it new thoughts and feelings, new aspirations and energies."

Beyond this remarkable justification of the study of history, and of the funding of its teaching at public expense, Turner was also expressing his own beliefs as to the uses of history. This essay was, as Professor Mood has noted, the statement of Turner's professional credo.[6] Having made this clear statement concerning the utility of history and of the necessity for each generation to rewrite history,

Turner was ready to present an essay outlining the role he would play in the process.

III *Problems in American History*

Turner's second important essay, "Problems in American History," appeared in the University of Wisconsin student newspaper in 1892; and although it is a very brief work, it is significant for several reasons. First of all, it identifies the areas which Turner felt offered the greatest opportunity for study in United States history. "American history," he contended, "needs a connected and unified account of the progress of civilization across this continent, with the attendant results." Future historians would have to study the "vital forces" which created and shaped the laws and institutions of the United States. There were many of these forces, Turner said, but the most outstanding was the fact that these institutions had been "compelled to adapt themselves to the changes of a remarkable developing, expanding people."[7] Moreover, it would be necessary to trace the development of many of these institutions: studies must be made of the extension of suffrage in the United States; of the history of the ballot; of the "growth of committee government in Congress"; of the government of territories; and of the "enlargement of the sphere of federal action by judicial decisions." These and many other areas would have to be investigated before a really acceptable history of the nation could be produced.

In this essay Turner first referred in print to the retreating frontier and to free land, thus at once identifying the fundamental economic factor which he later stressed in his interpretation of America and delineating the area of investigation that he had marked for his own.[8] "In a sense," he wrote, "American history up to our own day has been colonial history, the colonization of the great West. This ever retreating frontier of free land is the key to American development."

The study of history which Turner suggested in this essay went beyond the conventional bounds of historical activity. As he had suggested in "The Significance of History," history is past literature, politics, religion, and economics. The writing of history on such a vast scale, therefore, would demand the techniques and methods of other academic disciplines; it would require the skills of the geographer and the geologist, the cartographer, the political scientist.

What Turner was advocating was, therefore, the interdisciplinary approach which would be used widely by a later generation of historians. Had this essay been circulated among a larger, more academic audience, Turner rather than James Harvey Robinson might have been recognized as the father of the interdisciplinary method.

One other observation should be made about "Problems in American History": it presents evidence of the continuing development of ideas in Turner's mind. His review of Roosevelt's *Winning of the West* in the *Dial* had contained the first expression of Turner's interest in expansion as an important theme to be developed. "Problems in American History" adds to the concept of the retreating frontier and the continuing rebirth of civilization; and, in his third essay, "The Significance of the Frontier in American History," Turner presented the full expression of his interpretation of American history.

IV   *The Significance of the Frontier*

Turner was not, however, the first writer to stress "the most American of all explanations of the nation's distinctiveness." Almost from the founding of the country, Americans and Europeans alike had been aware that the frontier was a unique and potent force in the nation's development. Benjamin Franklin and Thomas Jefferson believed that the continuous movement of men westward slowed the growth of cities and strengthened the rural democracy, and the historian Francis Parkman believed that "contact with the wilderness endowed Europeans with 'a rugged independence. . . .' "[9] Alexis de Tocqueville saw American democracy as the result of the continuing exploitation of natural resources by the westward-moving population, and Lord Bryce must have had in mind a similar view when he wrote that "the West is the most American part of America." Karl Marx lamented that the American wage earner soon became an independent worker and thus was lost to the forces of labor.

The renowned editor of the *Nation,* Edwin L. Godkin, writing at the close of the Civil War, tied the frontier to basic American characteristics; and he suggested that "Democracy came from neither the [American] Revolution nor the decline of English nobility in America, but from the disruption of society as it moved Westward. . . ." These views, however, had but little impact on the American mind; the country was not ready to receive the frontier hypothesis.

An intellectual climate which was receptive to the frontier thesis developed, however, in the last two decades of the nineteenth century; and it was created in part by writers who realized that the impending exhaustion of free land would mark the end of an epoch in American history. Students looking for explanations for the depression of the 1890s also became aware that the frontier was closing, and they found in that fact subjects for articles which captured the popular interest. Thus, C. Wood Davis wrote in the *Country Gentleman* that the end of cheap land in the West was a panacea for the ills of the farmer and a catastrophe for the eastern worker who could no longer move westward to escape intolerable conditions. Other writers saw in the end of the frontier justification for halting the stream of southern European and Oriental emigrants whose growing numbers, racists believed, were a real threat to the nation. Such writing directed public attention to the role of the West in American history, and prepared the popular mind for the frontier thesis.

Nonetheless, the thesis which Turner outlined to the historians gathered in Chicago on that hot summer evening in 1893—the thesis which was to revolutionize the study and writing of history—developed naturally from his two shorter essays of 1891 and 1892. The theme of "The Significance of the Frontier in American History," that the recession of free land in the face of the advance of American settlement provided a key to understanding American development, had been suggested in "Problems in American History." Turner was ready, in 1893, to expand upon this idea.

Turner began his essay by quoting a statement of the superintendent of the census for 1890, which had appeared in a rather obscure government document in 1891: "Up to and including 1880 the country had a frontier of settlement, but at present the unsettled area has been so broken into by isolated bodies of settlement that there can hardly be said to be a frontier line. In the discussion of its extent, its westward movement, etc., it cannot, therefore, any longer have a place in the census reports."[10]

This statement, Turner asserted, "marks the closing of a great historic movement," because American history until that time had been in large part the history of the colonization of the Great West. American development could be traced through this process of colonization: "the existence of an area of free land, its continuous recession, and the advance of American settlement westward explain American development." This continuous expansion of the American people westward provided the "vital force" which called into existence the institutions and constitutional forms characteristic of the United States. But, in this progress of settlement across the continent, it has been necessary to make modification in their institutions, to adapt them to the needs and demands of the moment, whether those needs be connected with the problems of crossing the continent, subduing the wilderness, or facing the complexity of city life.

John C. Calhoun had put his finger on the distinguishing characteristic of American life, Turner believed, when he wrote in 1817 that "we are great and rapidly . . . growing." It was not just that the United States showed development; this was common to all nations. America had developed in unique and peculiar ways. It was high time that students of American history gave attention to what was unique; the germ theory of politics, which traced American institutions to an origin in the German forests, had been "sufficiently emphasized." This statement was a cavalier dismissal of the theory that had dominated historical thinking on the European continent and in the United States—a rash act by an undistinguished young historian which gave the lie to the official report that there was no place at this congress of historians for "sensational theorists."

The uniqueness of American development, the characteristics which distinguish Americans from Europeans, is explained not simply by the fact that American society had experienced an evolution of institutions but by the fact that this evolutionary process, occurring over a period of some three hundred years, had not been confined to a limited area. European peoples experienced this development within restricted geographical areas and always reached that point where additional development and expansion brought them into conflict with other peoples experiencing similar development. Inevitably, continual development and expansion required that the stronger nation conquer the weaker.

The United States was spared this stage of conflict because its evolutionary development occurred in a relatively unlimited physical area. This vast expanse of land added a new and unique dimension to American development. The evolutionary process recurred, with slightly different people and with slightly different institutions, at various stages of the movement across the continent. There was, Turner emphasized, "a recurrence of the process of evaluation in each Western area reached in the process of expansion." This reexamination meant that there was not simply a continuous development of American institutions and civilization as settlement moved ever westward. This process of development was regularly broken into, and a retrogressive stage of development followed a progressive one. Each new westward line of settlement repeated the process of settlement, from primitive institutions suitable for subduing the wilderness to the complex institutions necessary for life in a densely populated area.

But at no time were these repetitions of the developmental process identical. Each new wave of settlers which went to the frontier differed, however slightly, from the preceding frontiersmen, because each came from a different settled area. The character, nature, and extent of developmental progress which each settled area had achieved was affected by geographical and economic considerations, as well as by the composition and origin of the settlers. The West, all that land stretching from the line of settlement westward to the Pacific Ocean, had been the land of beginning again. "American social development has been continually beginning over again," Turner stated; and this "perennial rebirth, this fluidity of American life, this expansion westward with its new opportunities, its continuous touch with the simplicity of primitive society," were the "forces dominating American character." For this reason, Turner believed, the "true point of view in the history of this nation is not the Atlantic coast, it is the Great West." The major events in American history, Turner maintained, even such an event as the slavery controversy, achieved their importance because of their relation to westward expansion.

Thus did Turner shift his point of view from the traditional focus upon New England to the "Great West"; and, in doing so, he directed the historian's attention to the American phenomenon of continuous expansion. The outer edge of this advance, he said, was the frontier—that place where civilization meets savagery. It was now time, Turner believed, for Americans to give serious study to this meeting place—time for historians and economists to consider the American frontier as a major influence upon the shaping of American civilization.

Turner devoted the remainder of his essay to a consideration of the frontier. In introducing this theme, he made two statements which later critics all too often ignored. Addressing himself to the question of what the frontier is, Turner first made it clear that the traditional definition of the European frontier would not serve to explain the American one. The American frontier, he said, is not "a fortified boundary line running through dense populations" as do those on the Continent. The important thing is that it lies on the "hither edge" of free land; it is, in the usage of the census reports, "the margin of that settlement which has a density of two or more to the square mile. The term is an elastic one, and for our purposes does not need sharp definition." Despite this clear statement of the elasticity of the word "frontier", and his indication that a precise definition was not essential, Turner eventually was taken to task severely by critics who felt that he sometimes changed the meaning of the word.

The second statement made it clear that Turner did not regard his essay as a definitive treatment of the frontier. "This paper will make no attempt to treat the subject exhaustively," he wrote; "its aim is simply to call attention to the frontier as a fertile field for investigation, and to suggest some of the problems which arise in connection with it." There was no dogmatic assertation—no insistence—that he had hit upon *the* single satisfactory interpretation of American history. Yet the time would come when some scholars would accuse him of having done that very thing.

Having stated the aims and limitations of his essay, Turner concentrated upon the significance of the frontier in the development of American civilization. Early American history is the study of European germs developed in an American physical environment of European life, modified and developed by American forces. The first frontier, which ran along the Atlantic coast, was unquestionably a European frontier. But, as settlement moved westward, each successive frontier became more American and less European. It was on the frontier, Turner pointed out, that the "most rapid and effective Americanization" occurred. Here, in the first instance, the wilderness overcame the colonist. The colonist, European in dress, thought, and mode of travel, was "taken from the railroad car" and placed "on the birch canoe." He was stripped of the trappings of civilization and forced to regress to a primitive form of existence. Environment overcame civilization; and, to survive, man had to adapt himself to the conditions of the wilderness.

Eventually man was able to subdue partially the wilderness, and gradually the institutions of civilization were erected. But what resulted was not an old Europe, "not simply the development of Germanic germs," but "a new product that is American." Each successive frontier "leaves its traces behind it, and when it becomes a settled area, the region still partakes of the frontier characteristics." This process of growth has meant that each new line of frontier, each more westward outpost of settlement, was that much farther removed from European influence and was that much closer to becoming American civilization. The study of this advance, of the men who were a part of it, and of the institutions which they created was, for Turner, the really American part of American history.

Turner next considered the several types of frontier; and he dealt first with those marked by natural, or physical, boundaries: the fall line, just inland from the Atlantic coast, which separated the coastal plain from the gently rolling Piedmont; the Allegheny Mountains, which constituted the first formidable physical barrier to westward expansion; the Mississippi River; the Missouri River "where its direction approximates north and south"; the ninety-ninth meridian, which marks the beginning of the arid lands; and, finally, the Rocky Mountains. These, he said, had been the successive frontiers; and each of these temporary barriers had had its effect upon settlement in that area.

But Turner saw other frontiers which were identified by the people associated with them. Thus, there was the Indian-trader's frontier, the rancher's frontier, and, finally, the farmer's frontier. Each group, drawn to the unsettled area for reasons of exploitation, eventually succumbed partially to the next: the rancher pushed out the trader, only to have his area invaded by the farmer. Eventually, the press of population converted some of the farmland into towns and cities which were complete with manufacturing and with the complexities of developed civilization. Turner used the imagery of the poet as he described this process: "Stand at Cumberland Gap and watch the procession of civilization, marching single file—the buffalo, following the trail to the salt springs, the Indian, the fur-trader and hunter, the cattle-raiser, the pioneer farmer—and the frontier has passed by. Stand at South Pass in the Rockies a century

later and see the same procession with wider intervals between."
So, Turner concluded, "the United States lies like a huge page in
the history of society. Line by line as we read from west to east we
find the record of social evolution." In Turner's judgment, Achille
Loria, the Italian economist, was right when he had declared that
" 'America has the key to the historical enigma which Europe has
sought for centuries in vain, and the land which has no history
reveals luminously the course of universal history.' "[11]

Turner ended his essay with a consideration of the impact of the
frontier upon the process of civilization. First, the frontier "promoted the formation of a composite nationality for the American
people." While the Atlantic coast was settled by Englishmen, it was
continental immigration which pushed beyond the original settlements. The Scotch-Irish, those frontiersmen *par excellence,* and the
Palatine Germans, known as the Pennsylvania Dutch, had settled
and populated the colonial frontier. With these settlers had come
the redemptioners, the free indentured servants, frequently of
non-English origin. All these diverse people, in the "crucible of the
frontier . . . were Americanized, liberated, and fused into a mixed
race, English in neither nationality nor characteristics." This process of amalgamation, which Tocqueville had considered significant,
"has gone on from the early days to our own."

A second effect of the frontier was economic. It stimulated the
growth of manufacturing and gave rise to the development of a
diversified agriculture to supply the needs of the growing and ur-
banizing eastern United States. Moreover, with the expansion of
population in the frontier areas, eastern seaboard cities such as
Baltimore, Boston, and New York competed for what George
Washington called " 'the extensive and valuable trade of a rising
empire.' "[12]

The development of nationalism and the breakdown of sectionalism were fostered by the frontier. Much of the legislation
which developed the power of the national government—public-
land policy, tariff policy, internal improvement—was influenced by
the expanding frontier. "The growth of nationalism and the evolution of American political institutions," said Turner, "were depen-
dent on the advance of the frontier." This nationalizing tendency of
the West "transformed the democracy of Jefferson into the national
republicanism of Monroe and the democracy of Andrew Jackson."
"Mobility of population is death to localism," Turner pointed out;

"and the western frontier worked irresistibly in unsettling population."

But the most important effect of the frontier was its promotion of democracy. The primitive organization of society on the frontier encouraged self-reliance and independence. This frontier society was antisocial, opposed to any forms of control; it gloried in personal liberty and individualism. Turner maintained that this "frontier individualism has from the beginning promoted democracy." Indeed, the western states, entering the Union in the first quarter-century of the new nation's life, brought more democratic suffrage provisions; and western parts of such states as New York and Virginia demanded and secured democratic voting policies in state constitutions. And democracy as an effective force came into government at the national level with the appearance of such western leaders as Andrew Jackson and William Henry Harrison. This rise of democracy, Turner declared, was the "triumph of the frontier—with all of its good and with all of its evil elements."

The vigor with which western politicians pursued democracy and the tendency of westerners sometimes to equate individual liberty with an absence of effective government were alarming to easterners. They understood as well as westerners that, "so long as free land exists, the opportunity for a competency exists, and economic power secures political power." Therefore, attempts were made to regulate and control the frontier and its inhabitants. Schemes to halt or to slow the process of westward expansion and to regulate the acquisition of land were unsuccessful. Only the religious and educational activities which easterners undertook in the West enjoyed any real success in regulating the frontier. But the frontier affected these religious and intellectual areas as much as it was affected by them.

With democracy came opportunity, and "escape from the bondage of the past; . . . freshness, and confidence, and scorn of older society, impatience of its restraints and its ideas, and indifference to its lessons, have accompanied the frontier. What the Mediterranean Sea was to the Greeks . . . that, and more, the ever retreating frontier has been to the United States."[13] So, Turner concluded, "four centuries from the discovery of America, at the end of a hundred years of life under the Constitution, the frontier is gone, and with its going has closed the first period of American history."

The frontier thesis did not spring full-blown from any sudden inspiration which came to Turner's mind; it resulted from his personal experiences as a youth growing up close to the line of frontier and from his keen awareness of the stimulating intellectual activity which was swirling about the country in the last quarter of the nineteenth century. Turner was a part of all this activity; he never allowed himself to be confined within narrow lines of academic departmentalization but always ranged freely throughout the entire area of intellectual activity; and always he had a probing mind and an insatiable curiosity. Ever alert to the possibility of gaining insight into his own historical interests through knowledge and techniques used in other disciplines, he read widely in, and borrowed freely from, developments in all segments of scholarly endeavor. He had been introduced to the doctrine of evolution and its utility in the study of history by Professor Allen, and he was aware of the intellectual ferment in religion, of the increasing activity of reformers and of reform groups, and of the strain and tests which a rapidly growing population placed upon the concepts of democracy. He wrote often for the general public and always he maintained an interest in what was "in the air"—the hopes, the aspirations, and the objectives which the American people had for their nation. Turner was influenced by all of these factors, and all of them played a part in his development of the frontier hypothesis. Ultimately, most of them—religion, reform, the American concept of democracy—were influenced by him.

The immediate response to "The Significance of the Frontier in American History" was, as already noted, less than enthusiastic; at best, it was polite and perfunctory. This absence of enthusiasm for, or opposition to, the thesis is explained by several factors. In the first place, the ideas which Turner presented ran contrary to the prevailing interpretation of American history; for "the current vogue" in historical circles was, as Gene M. Gressley has noted, "the 'germ' school" which had been popularized by Herbert Baxter Adams at Johns Hopkins. A novel interpretation by a young and relatively unknown professor from a midwestern university was not likely to attract much attention or provoke much comment among professional historians. For another thing, the audience in Chicago was not large, and later in the year, when Turner read his paper at a meeting of the State Historical Society of Wisconsin, the audience was also small. His earlier essays had suffered under the same handicap since they had appeared in the University of Wisconsin's education extension journal and in the undergraduate newspaper. Finally, an essay so filled with thought-provoking ideas could hardly be grasped at first reading; time would be required to digest its meaning and to comprehend its true significance. In the meantime, these ideas had to be exposed to a wider audience.

V *Popularizing the Thesis*

Turner himself was responsible for popularizing the concepts which he had advanced in "The Significance of the Frontier in American History," and he did so by producing a fairly steady stream of articles and essays, some of which were designed specifically to catch the popular interest. In the year following the Chicago address, Turner authored an entry entitled "Frontier" in a new edition of *Johnson's Universal Cyclopaedia*, a publication which enjoyed a respectable readership, and the article, which carried his name, provided an opportunity for Turner to expand his discussion of the frontier.[14]

Turner's attempt to popularize the frontier hypothesis met with particular success with his publication of "The Problem of the West," which appeared in the September, 1896, issue of the *Atlantic Monthly*.[15] This essay, which presented a clear restatement of the hypothesis, emphasized especially the problems which the United States faced "as the pioneering era drew to a close. . . ."[16] Appearing in the momentous election year of 1896, the essay seemed to provide some "meaning to the turbulent politics of the 1890's; only by understanding America's pioneering past could modern Americans understand the East-West divisions that governed political behavior."[17] So well did the frontier thesis seem to provide answers to the problems of the day that the essay was reprinted in *Public Opinion* and summarized or written about in newspapers from coast to coast. The Chicago *Tribune*, that booster of the Midwest, "found in the essay striking proof that national problems could be sensibly resolved only by entrusting political power to 'the half-dozen states grouped about Chicago.' "[18] The Boston *Herald*, viewing the scene in New England's rarefied atmosphere, saw in Turner's words "the first reasonable explanation for the wild-eyed Populists who were attempting to capture the Presidency for free silver and anarchy. Here . . . 'is the effort of a new force to find expression.' "[19]

The popular success which Turner achieved with "The Problem

of the West" was repeated in several of his articles that appeared in the following months: "Dominant Forces in American Life"; "The Middle West"; and "Contributions of the West to American Democracy."[20] In the meantime, the original essay, "The Significance of the Frontier in American History," appeared in several historical journals as well as in the yearbook of the National Herbart Society in 1899 and in the *International Socialist Review* in 1905. Such advertising was, as Ray Allen Billington has pointed out, "first-rate advertising indeed," for Turner and for the frontier thesis.[21]

VI   *Turner's Growing Reputation*

The publicity generated by these essays and by the reprinting of the frontier thesis soon placed Professor Turner in the front rank of American historians. He became a sought-after speaker at meetings of scholarly groups and was soon well known among the American intellectual community. His engaging personality made him welcome to every group, and the number of his friends and contacts expanded greatly. As his work became recognized by an ever-widening audience, he was asked increasingly to write reviews of new publications in the field of history. Thus, he became an active reviewer for the *Atlantic Monthly*, the *Political Science Quarterly*, and the *Dial*, as well as a regular contributor of reviews to the *American Historical Review*. In addition to his essays and reviews which appeared with increasing frequency, Turner found time to edit a number of documents dealing with foreign affairs during the American Revolution. This work, which was done for the Historical Manuscripts Commission of the American Historical Association, brought Turner into close contact with J. Franklin Jameson, Talcott Williams, William P. Trent, and James Bain, Jr., all of them influential leaders of the historical profession. Thus, by the beginning of the new century, Turner "was a member of the inner circle of historians who ran the American Historical Association."[22]

Turner's services were also sought in other ways. He received offers from many universities which desired to enhance their prestige by adding to their faculties the man Woodrow Wilson later called " 'the coming man in American history.' "[23] One of the most appealing of these offers came from Princeton University and was proffered by Turner's friend from his Johns Hopkins days, Wilson himself, who in 1890 had become a professor at that venerable institution.[24] Turner realized the advantages to be derived from being associated with an old and distinguished university and from contact with literary and intellectual activity of the East, and he was certain that it would be pleasant to have Wilson as a colleague. On the other hand, he realized the value of the research facilities at Wisconsin, he was comfortably situated there, and he had made a place for himself on the Wisconsin faculty. His letters to Wilson reveal his reluctance to leave, and it was perhaps fortunate that the anticipated chair in history was not established at this time by Princeton's trustees.[25]

The reputation which Turner gained in the last years of the century benefited him in additional ways. Aspiring students, as much as established scholars, were attracted to the man and his ideas. As a result, students from all parts of the United States descended upon the Madison campus and enrolled in Turner's seminars. Because of this rapidly increasing enrollment, because of his prestige on the campus, and because of his talent for vigorous leadership and organization Turner converted his Department of History into the School of Economics, Political Science and History, which by the end of the century had earned a distinguished reputation for the quality of its graduate instruction.

The new-frontier theme proved a godsend to popular writers and lecturers who were soon extolling the virtues of the indomitable frontiersman or glorifying the frontier itself as "the central and determining fact of our national history."[26] Typical was John Fiske, a popular lecturer in the last years of the century, who, in 1895, was giving an address on "The Influence of the Frontier Upon American Life."[27] Finally, the writers of textbooks, now that the frontier had become respectable, could enliven their writing with exciting stories of life on the frontier—ones replete with colorful, brave, and resourceful heroes. "The West," as an outstanding student of Turner and the frontier has noted, "began to push constitutional details from schoolbooks."[28]

VII   Acceptance of the Frontier Thesis

By 1906, when *Rise of the New West, 1819–1829* appeared, Turner was a major historian whose thesis had won general acclaim. A variety of factors helped explain this widespread acceptance of Turner's concept of the frontier. First, as Gene Gressley has noted, the "age was ripe for a nationalistic explanation of America's growth."[29] Americans were aware, and proud, of the development they had achieved; but the end of the nineteenth century found them standing somewhat uncertainly on the world stage in the unfamiliar character of a major power. How had they arrived there? What characteristics, what attributes, had enabled a relative handful of persons, loosely organized into a nation, to attain such marvelous development in little more than a hundred years? Turner's explanation, that a key to understanding this amazing growth lay in the people themselves and in the American environment, sounded a pleasing note and struck a responsive chord in his fellow Americans. Certainly they would embrace an explanation which located the genius of America's growth in themselves and on their continent. They, too, were ready to cast aside the traditional explanation that traced their success to Europe and Europeans. Moreover, the emphasis of the role of the frontier coincided with the remarkable shift of interest and power from the East coast toward the Pacific. The West had vigorously challenged the East in the presidential campaign of 1896; and the frontier thesis, particularly as Turner had outlined it in "The Problem of the West," seemed both to chronicle and explain western growth.

A second reason for the acceptance of the frontier theory was found in the growth of evolutionary doctrines. Such concepts, originally used to explain biological development, were increasingly being considered as helpful devices to trace the developmental processes in other academic areas. The very fact that Turner had employed this modern and scientific concept perhaps enhanced the rightness of his conclusions, at least in the minds of the better-educated portion of the population.

Third, the last decade of the old century had witnessed a remarkable increase of interest in history—one that had developed, in large measure, at the grass-roots level. This interest was evidenced by the organization of a large number of state historical societies, by a growing interest in genealogy, and by the opening of libraries and museums in towns and cities in all parts of the United States. An attempt to recall and to record the local past resulted in the appearance of many state and county histories, particularly in those regions west of the Allegheny-Appalachian chain. Thus, an intellectual climate was created which was highly receptive to the Turner thesis. What Turner had done for the frontier, others could attempt to do for a smaller area. Therefore, Gressley concludes, "each historian in

his own bailiwick was provided with a historical theory upon which
to test his personal observations, and in so doing he was given the
feeling of contributing to the interpretation of his nation."[30]

But, fourth, Turner's students were primarily responsible for the
widespread acceptance of the frontier thesis; for few teachers have
exerted so much influence upon students as Turner did in his seminars. In these meetings, stimulation came from student and teacher
alike; Turner—charming, gracious, and encouraging thoughtful
criticism of his ideas and those of his students—seemed to learn as
much from his students as they from him. Perhaps this exposure to
his magnetic personality, as much as to the ideas which he presented, won for him the unswerving loyalty of students who studied
in his seminars. Whatever the cause, these young men and women
exhibited a devotion to Turner and to his ideas which only grew
stronger after they left the Madison campus. "A high percentage of
them," Gressley points out, "consecrated their lives to exploring the
unknowns of the 'hither edge.' "[31]

Moreover, Professor Turner trained a large number of scholars,
both at the University of Wisconsin and later at Harvard; and they,
too, went forth to "preach the gospel" and to establish the Turnerian
tradition at major schools in all parts of the United States. By the
time Turner's *Rise of the New West* appeared, disciples had established themselves on many important western campuses: "Joseph
Schafer was at Oregon, Edmond Meany at Washington, Clark at
Texas, Hibbard at Ames, Libby at North Dakota, Becker at Kansas."[32] In 1910, when Turner resigned from the University of Wisconsin faculty, he could point with pride to a large number of his
"seminarians"—Herbert E. Bolton, Guy Stanton Ford, Carl Lotus
Becker, Homer C. Hockett, and Solon J. Buck, among others—
whose publications had raised them to positions of prominence in
the historical profession. Equally impressive was the number of
Turner's students who served as president of the American Historical Association. In view of this activity, there can be little doubt
about Professor Gressley's statement: "If Professor Turner had
never written a word his concepts would have been well-known
through the publicizing of his students."[33]

By the time Turner moved to Harvard, the frontier hypothesis
was firmly established—it was widely known and generally accepted. Turner's vigorous intellect was now moving in another direction: he became concerned with another force, sectionalism,

which he felt was essential to a clear understanding of American history. The nation and its sections dominated the remainder of his professional activity, and this new direction in his thinking was first presented in *The Rise of the New West, 1819–1829.*

CHAPTER 3

The Sectional Hypothesis

I Rise of the New West

TURNER'S *Rise of the New West, 1819–1829* was published by
Harper and Brothers in 1906 as the fourteenth volume in the
American Nation Series. A transitional book, it linked the frontier
hypothesis of Turner's early fame with his later theory of the role of
sections in the history of the United States. By the time this volume
appeared, the frontier thesis had been generally accepted; and
Turner no longer felt it necessary to publicize the theory. Instead,
he stated it at this time primarily as an introduction, a very important introduction, to the new concept of sectionalism which he presented in his book. This concept, which occupied the remainder of
his professional life, he more clearly expressed later in two essays,
"Significance of Sections in American History" and "Sections and
Nation." Therefore, *Rise of the New West* was actually Turner's "last
serious effort to illustrate the role of the frontier in American history."[1]

II Difficulty in Writing the Book

That the *Rise of the New West* was the only book to come from the
pen of this brilliant man in his own lifetime is better understood
when one realizes the mental and physical agonies Turner suffered
in completing the work. The book (but not the concept—Turner for
some years had been studying the role of sections as a force in
American development) had had its beginnings as early as 1899. In
that year the American Historical Association, in an effort to inject
some vitality into the study and writing of American history, ap-
pointed a committee to develop plans for a monographic history of
the United States. The association envisaged a series of books cover-
ing the entire scope of American history, and each was to be written
by a specialist in his particular field, and each was to employ both

scientific method and recent research findings. Despite the fact that Turner was not yet forty years of age, his eminent position as a professional historian dictated that he should have a place on the committee, together with Charles Francis and Herbert Baxter Adams, William Dunning, John Bach McMaster, and Moses Coit Tyler. Professor Albert Bushnell Hart of Harvard, who chaired the committee and became editor of the series,[2] persuaded Turner to accept the assignment of preparing one of the volumes; and Hart, who had remarkable perseverance, finally extracted the completed manuscript from Turner's reluctant hands.

From the outset, Turner questioned the wisdom of permitting himself to contribute a volume to the undertaking. Nor was he certain that he should even become involved in the enterprise as an advisor. Writing to his friend J. Franklin Jameson in 1900, Turner confessed that he knew "nothing of the matter" of the "co-op" history, and he confided that he doubted the "wisdom of mixing up my ideas with other peoples."[3] Despite Turner's doubts Hart was determined that he would have a volume from Turner. "Yours was one of the first names to occur to my mind as fundamental in any scheme of cooperative scholarship in American history," Hart wrote in his letter offering Turner virtually his choice of the more than thirty volumes then projected for the series.[4] This flattering approach had little effect on Turner; he already had contracts to fulfill; and he was not satisfied with the flat fee of fifteen hundred dollars which the authors for the series were to receive. Moreover, at the moment he was engrossed in source materials relating to the diplomatic history of the United States prior to the purchase of the Louisiana Territory, and he wanted to complete this work.[5]

But Hart, not to be refused, went to Madison to press his case; and he told Turner, among other things, that "the men of history and the world of letters were entitled to something from you and something soon."[6] Turner began to weaken, although, as he wrote to Jameson, he prayed "not to be led into temptation."[7] Temptation overcame him, and Turner wrote Hart on March 8, 1902, that he would do the volume on the New West.[8]

This decision marked the beginning of one of the most painful periods in Turner's life, for writing was always an unpleasant task for him. His great joy was in seeking out new information, in developing new interpretations, in presenting hypotheses. After the new material had been unearthed and the interpretation of it formed,

Turner found little satisfaction in recording it in scholarly fashion. The thrill, for him, was in the search for additional information, not in its exposition. Besides, he never was really ready to write: there always was yet another bit of information needed, or another insight which required additional research, thought, and study. The job he had to do was disagreeable from first to last, and it demanded all his thought and energy. Even his seminars and classes were devoted largely to developing material for the book; his lectures became pages of manuscript; every waking moment was devoted to study and writing about the New West. In spite of all his effort, he made little headway, not because words came slowly, but because he could not stop thinking about what he had written; and this thinking suggested new approaches that required additional study.

The deadline for delivery of the manuscript, March, 1905, came and went. Letters from Hart arrived more frequently, each more insistent than the last. Hart encouraged, cajoled, and chided but all to little avail. For his part, Turner worked furiously, but the end was not in sight. Finally, Hart pointed out that Turner's failure to complete his manuscript threatened to hold up completion of the series. "Your volume," he wrote Turner in July, "is becoming the needle's eye for the series."[9] Turner labored all through the summer of 1905: he wrote a paragraph and then went outside to smoke a cigarette and walk around the house while forming, in his mind, the next paragraph to be written.[10]

Finally, Turner's labor and Hart's prodding resulted in a completed manuscript. Turner was able to write to his wife on December 7, 1905, "Finished my rough draft of last chapter today."[11] But much remained to be done. The draft was much too long, and there remained the task of compiling the bibliography and correcting the manuscript. A printable copy finally was ready for the publishers in January, 1906, after a flurry of work which kept Turner away from the annual meeting of the American Historical Association and which gave rise to an occasional flaring of tempers by the author and the editor. It had been a trying time for both men; and Hart, recalling the experience shortly after Turner's death, wrote their mutual friend, Max Farrand, "It ought to be carved on my tombstone . . . that I was the only man in the world that secured what might be called an adequate volume from Turner."[12]

The product of this anguish was, however, well worth its cost to both Hart and Turner. The *Rise of the New West* was a "fresh breeze in American historical writing." The style was "modern, crisp, factual," with brilliant, "epitomizing phrases."[13] It was a new style of historical writing, a style well suited to the purposes which the American Historical Association had had in mind when it had launched the cooperative history. Nonetheless, Turner had faced formidable problems in the organization of the volume. The fact that he had to deal with the entire scope of United States history for the decade 1819–1829 led him rather naturally to a consideration of sections and to the role they had played in the nation's history; and this consideration aided him greatly in solving some of the literary problems which he faced.

Thus, the first eight chapters (less a brief introductory chapter, "Nationalism and Sectionalism [1815–1830]"), or approximately half of the book, are devoted to the several sections composing the United States during that decade. In these chapters, appropriately, the style is expository and descriptive. The remaining eleven chapters, narrative in style, deal with the course of American history during the period and are entitled "The Crisis of 1819 and Its Results," "The Missouri Compromise," "Party Politics," "The Monroe Doctrine," "Internal Improvements," "The Tariff of 1824," "The Election of 1824," "President Adams and the Opposition," and "Internal Improvements and Foreign Trade." The volume concludes with a consideration of the reaction toward state sovereignty, the tariff of abominations, and the South Carolina exposition and protest. Thus, as Professor Turner concluded, the book dealt with the process of transformation; "beginning with nationalism, the period ends with sectionalism."[14]

In order to understand the period covered by the book, Turner pointed out, it was necessary to "determine what were the main interests shown in each [section] and impressed upon the leaders who represented them"; for, as he concluded in his introductory chapter,

. . . in the minds of some of the most enlightened statesmen of this decade, American politics were essentially a struggle for power between rival sections.

Even those of most enlarged national sympathies and purposes accepted the fact of sectional rivalries and combinations as fundamental in their policies.[15]

National policy, as stated in tariff measures, in foreign policy, in internal improvements, was what resulted when compromise and conciliation "reduced the originally extreme claims of rival sections to a decent moderation."[16] Thus Turner saw sections injecting through their several champions in the halls of congress those issues best designed to advance their own interests; these conflicting sectional interests were modified through mighty congressional debates and finally emerged as national policy.

But there was one other change which had to be presented, one which was not readily revealed by the examination of the American sections. "This," said Turner, "was the formation of the self-conscious American democracy, strongest in the West and middle regions, but running across all sections and tending to divide the people on the lines of social classes. This democracy came into its own when Andrew Jackson triumphed over the old order of things and rudely threw open the sanctuary of federal government to the populace."[17]

To characterize the several sections, indicate their influence upon national affairs, trace the general development of American history through the period covered, and indicate the rise of "self-conscious democracy" within an acceptable literary framework were frightening tasks at best. The job was made more difficult by the limitations of space imposed by the editor. Turner was unable to elaborate upon some points which deserved extended treatment, and some topics which he wanted to consider had been reserved for other volumes.[18]

It is not surprising, therefore, that *Rise of the New West* was not quite the polished volume which many historians had expected from their brilliant colleague. Contemporary reviewers indicated this feeling at the same time that they bestowed upon it a generally warm acceptance.[19] Writing more recently, a keen student of American history has pointed out that "the over-all effect [of the book] is disappointing, . . . parts of it become a mere compendium of facts" and his "individuals tend to be stereotypes: Clay and Jackson were the West, John Quincy Adams was New England, and, all too often, John Randolph, crabby and schizophrenic, was the South."[20]

Despite these criticisms and the weaknesses upon which they were based, *Rise of the New West* "revolutionized the interpretation of early American history."[21] Its methodology and its conclusions proved to be highly persuasive; and the findings presented in the volume soon became commonplace, "enshrined in textbooks read by generations of college students."[22] Writing in a Foreword to a reissue of the book which appeared in 1962, Ray Allen Billington, himself an eminent writer about the American West, noted that in the half century since its original publication *Rise of the New West* had come to be recognized "as one of the major classics of American historical writing."[23]

Nor was Billington alone in his appraisal; he was joined by other able historians who both praised the work and suggested reasons for its lasting influence upon American historiography. Avery Craven asserted that *Rise of the New West* would "retain its place as a sound, scholarly production by the best modern tests long after most of the volumes in the American Nation series have lost their standing and their place on select library shelves. And it will do so because of its firm grip on the fundamental forces which were at work in shaping the nation's course in its period."[24] And, finally, Fulmer Mood, writing in 1939, offered this explanation for the significance of the volume: "The book sums up and gives permanent expression to Turner's individual genius for historiography. It is the perfect and perfected flowering of his own special method of historical workmanship, displayed in all its many-sided richness and exacting refinement. As a historical construction it is utterly novel in its ordonnance, a supremely difficult feat excellently performed."[25]

This volume, then, was the stage from which Turner launched his second hypothesis. Certainly in this book he had a more effective means of introducing his sectional thesis than that employed to present the frontier thesis. The idea would be further developed, however, principally in two essays published in his lifetime and in a book which appeared posthumously.

III *The Significance of Sections*

Turner wrote in 1922 that some fifteen years earlier he began to urge the importance of the section in American history, "perhaps because the contemporary significance of the frontier was declining. . . ."[26] He made it clear, however, that his interest in the role played by sections in American history had been contemporaneous with his study of the frontier. Frontier and section were, he believed, "mutually interpretative," and "no one could follow the advance of settlement . . . and fail to see the evolution of new Sections [sic]."[27] So he undertook a study of the several traditional regions, or sections, in the United States—the Old Northwest, the Middle West, the Western Border states, the Old Southwest—and, finally, the newer sections which resulted from the nineteenth-century westward advance: the New Southwest, the New Northwest, the Pacific coast region, the Great Plains, and the Rocky Mountains. His study of these regions, to which he devoted most of his professional life, convinced him that sections had played a prominent role indeed in the development of the United States.

Sectionalism, which came with the first settlers to the Atlantic coast, arose from the differing physical characteristics of the lands first settled; and it was early nurtured by the different peoples and types of society which composed these early settlements. But these earliest sections, bordering on the Atlantic Ocean, were soon modified by the force of movement. The westward movement, with its constant "beginning over again," meant that the country, throughout the nineteenth century, was at the same time both a developed and a primitive society. Mature and newly developing regions obviously had different objectives and different needs; their individual state of development and their physical environment dictated that they would think of themselves, and of the nation, in different ways. The West, wherever it was located geographically in any given year, was agricultural, only slightly populated, in need of capital, and composed chiefly of the self-sufficient family as the economic unit. The East, more densely populated, more urban and industrial, possessed a complex social organization and was the creditor region of the country. The frontier section stressed the rights of man while the spokesmen for the East emphasized the rights of property.

Clearly, then, both frontier and section existed from the earliest days of settlement on the eastern seaboard. Just as clearly, the existence of sections, with their differing needs and desires, inspired sectional rivalry. Indeed, Turner noted that the whole process of westward advance was "an advance of rival sections, Northeastern, Middle and Southern."[28] Each section distrusted the other, and with good reason. The West believed in rule by the majority—in control by what John Randolph of Virginia called "King Numbers." The western man was optimistic, reckless, and innovative; the eastern man feared the effect of unbridled democracy on minority and property rights, and he held "innovation" to be a term of reproach. Eastern apprehension of the expansive and buoyant frontiersman was voiced as early as 1787 when Gouverneur Morris of Pennsylvania urged the Constitutional Convention to "so fix the ratio of representation that the number of representatives from the Atlantic States should always be larger than the number from the Western States."[29]

Here, then, was the first great conflict between sections, that between East and West; and the westward expansion advanced the rivalry of sections simply because the West represented opportunity for the sections which had early developed close to the Atlantic coast. As an eastern section advanced inland, it acquired additional resources; it sent there its own people to spread the gospel—the beliefs, ideologies, and desires—of its own region; and it placed itself in a position where it could guide and direct these people through the process of achieving statehood, thus adding materially to the political influence of the older section. Soon, therefore, the Northeast, the Middle Section, and the South were competing in the process of western settlement.

Soon, too, other elements of sectional rivalry were added— economic considerations, internal improvements, tariff questions—and the newly settled regions themselves, operating under their own unique physical circumstances, developed regional interests and concerns—protection from Indians, federal subsidy for transportation, cheap money; and the natural outcome was the development of regional, or sectional, self-consciousness. One after another, the more westward sections became, not the extensions of eastern sections as had been hoped, but independent sections with their own personality, advancing their causes against the Northeast, the Middle section, and the South indiscriminately. The United States had become a nation of sections.

But Turner meant by the term "section" something other than that which is generally meant by the word. "To the average American," he wrote, "to most American historians, and to most of the writers of our school textbooks . . . the word *section* applies only to the struggle of South against North on the questions of slavery, state sovereignty, and, eventually, disunion. But the Civil War was only the most drastic and most tragic of sectional manifestations. . . ."[30] This conflict, Turner stated, was not what the word meant to him; section referred to "the more complicated and various sectionalism which has run through American development."[31]

To understand the section, in the all-encompassing scope which

Turner assigned it, meant the acquisition of detailed knowledge of the social, political, economic, geographic, and hereditary factors which existed within a region. Turner's study of the role of sections in the history of the United States clearly reflected his acceptance of the theory of multiple causation; he felt no constraint to work exclusively within his own academic discipline when the methods or facts of other scholarly areas might shed light upon his problem.[32] With this meaning of the word in mind, it becomes easier to understand how Turner could amass dozens of file cabinets containing thousands of note cards and yet produce only a brief list of major publications.

For Turner, the section provided a manageable and meaningful approach to the study of American history. "The United States means much more than a single country," he wrote. "It is too large to treat as a unit." He pointed out that the country was too large and various to be seen as an entity. He cited the numerous European visitors to the United States who, having seen a few major cities, or having glimpsed the western landscape from a moving train, felt prepared to write descriptive volumes of the nation; and natives erred in the same manner. Each man tended to think of America in terms of his own region; to see the nation "as his section writ large."[33] No wonder it was difficult for Americans to understand one another, or to agree on what policies were best for the nation!

Turner saw an analogy to the American sections in European nations. "The significance of the section in American history," he wrote, "is that it is the faint image of a European nation and that we need to reexamine our history in the light of this fact. Our politics and our society have been shaped by sectional complexity and interplay not unlike what goes on between European nations."[34] Students of American history tend to think of their country in much the same way that they think of one of the nations of Europe, but a clearer understanding might be gained by realizing that there is real similarity between the United States and Europe itself. The sheer size of the United States renders impossible any real comparison with an individual European nation. As Turner pointed out in "Sections and Nation," England, France, and Italy could be contained within the area of the original thirteen states; and the Middle West could hold all the European powers which joined Germany in World War I. When size was considered, then, the section assumed new importance; for, when we recall that each major section of the nation "has its own geographical qualities, its own resources and economic capacities, and its own rival interests," the similarity between the American section and the European nation becomes more obvious. "The American section may be likened to the shadowy image of the European nation," Turner said, "to the European state denatured of its toxic qualities."[35]

If, then, we conceive of American sections in this light—if we think of the United States as a land of several "nations"—we may wonder how America avoided, with one tragic exception, the warfare so characteristic of Europe. Turner maintains that we have done so because "we substituted the system of a sectional union and legislative adjustment, for the settlement by the sword. . . . Like an elastic band, the common national feeling and party ties draw sections together, but at the same time yield in some measure to sectional interests when these are gravely threatened."[36]

We have provided for Europe [Turner concludes], the example of a continental federation of sections over an area equal to Europe itself, and by substituting discussion and concession and compromised legislation for force, we have shown the possibility of international political parties, international legislative bodies, and international peace. Our party system and our variety in regional geography have helped to preserve the American peace.

The thing to be avoided, if the lessons of history are followed, is the insistence upon the particular interests and ideals of the section in which we live, without sympathetic comprehension of the ideals, the interests, and rights of other sections. We must shape our national action to the fact of a vast and varied Union of unlike sections.[37]

During the years that Turner was occupied with research on the sectional hypothesis, he was also engaged in other aspects of his academic career; and it was during these same years that he achieved his greatest recognition. In the years following publication of *Rise of the New West,* he experienced increasing dissatisfaction with the University of Wisconsin's board of regents, a dissatisfaction which led to his decision, in 1909, to resign his position at Wisconsin and accept a chair at Harvard University. In 1910, he began a term as president of the American Historical Association; and, following the publication of his presidential address, "Social Forces in

American History," in the January, 1911, number of the *American Historical Review*, he became less active as a writer but continued to devote himself intensely to research and teaching.

IV *Involvement in Campus Politics*

Turner's growing national reputation and his keen judgment of people led to his involvement in University of Wisconsin campus politics and university decision-making. By 1900 he had become a powerful figure on the campus and, after his work in 1901 and 1902 to secure the university presidency for Charles R. Van Hise, he was sometimes referred to as a "president-maker." Much of his time was spent on committee work and as an official representative of the university. The faculty and administration tended to "lionize" Turner, and to seek both his advice and his services as a spokesman for the faculty. In this latter capacity, Turner became involved in a movement to curtail the trend toward professionalism in intercollegiate football which was noticeable on midwestern university campuses by 1905.

As chairman of a faculty committee established to eliminate professionalism in athletics, Turner found himself conducting voluminous correspondence with colleagues at other midwestern universities. In the attempt to remove from regional schools such powerful coaches as Alonzo Stagg of the University of Chicago and Field H. Yost of the University of Michigan, Turner had the aid of Albion W. Small at Chicago; James A. Jones, a former student of Turner's, at Northwestern; and Albert H. Pattengill at Michigan. Despite their best efforts, little reform of athletics was accomplished; and Turner, by 1906, decided to drop the time-consuming affair.[38]

By 1908, Turner was facing increasing criticism from the university's board of regents. The regents' dissatisfaction probably stemmed from an arrangement they had made with Turner in 1906 when Turner had almost accepted a position at Stanford University after having declined persistent offers from the universities of California and Chicago. Although the California earthquake of that year produced such damage on the Stanford campus that the university, faced with unanticipated expenditures for rebuilding, was forced to postpone its invitation to Turner, it was generally known at Wisconsin that Turner had definitely decided to make the move to Stanford. Because of these offers, attempts were made to retain Turner at Wisconsin; and the regents offered him the inducement of a reduced teaching load.

How little this body understood the nature of Turner's work, and the strength of his commitment to it, is illustrated in the memorandum presented for Turner's approval: "In order that Professor J. F. Turner may carry to a conclusion the very important investigations in history upon which he has been engaged for many years, and put the results of the same into form for publication [it is resolved] that he be relieved from instructional work for such part of one semester in each year as may be necessary to that end. . . ."[39] If the regents were expecting completion of research and publication of his findings in the not too distant future, as perhaps they were, Turner soon disabused them of such expectation. He accepted the memorandum, but he deleted the words "to a conclusion" and substituted the words "advantageously carry on."[40]

The regents were impatient with this one-semester-leave arrangement by 1908, and they suggested that so much time spent in research indicated a lack of interest in his students and in the instructional program of the university. At the request of President Charles Richard Van Hise, Turner prepared a report on students of his who had won the coveted Justin Winsor Prize, an annual award made by the American Historical Association for the best unpublished monograph in American history. This report was used by Van Hise to defend both Turner's own research activities and the university's policy of encouraging research. In the report, Turner indicated that Wisconsin had produced more productive scholars than those who had won the Winsor prize, but he disclaimed exclusive credit for the success of these students. He expressed the belief, however, that much of their success could be attributed to Wisconsin's emphasis upon research, a point of view which, he noted, already had come to be referred to as the "Wisconsin School." Turner also included in this report an indication of the status assigned him by some former students, now distinguished historians themselves. He noted that he had received a book, *Westward Extension*, by George P. Garrison, head of the Department of History at the University of Texas, inscribed "To the master of Western history."[41]

Evidently, President Van Hise felt additional ammunition was needed in the battle with the regents, because he asked Turner in the same year for a report on the progress of his research. To submit a scholar of Turner's distinction to the onerous task of preparing a work-progress report must have been an extremely disagreeable experience for both men. Van Hise was both an outstanding scholar himself and a close personal friend of Turner, and he was dedicated to encouraging research and scholarship at the university; and for Turner, who was aware of his growing reputation as a scholar who had received impressive invitations from many universities anxious to add him to their faculties, the request must have represented a frightful indignity. Nevertheless, the report was prepared and presented. Seemingly, the unpleasantness of his last years at Wisconsin, which he described to a friend as being "a kind of night-mare to me," left no rancor toward the school; however, it did influence Turner's decision to accept the offer from Harvard.[42]

V *Offers from Other Institutions*

Almost from the time he announced his frontier thesis at Chicago in 1893, Professor Turner had been the recipient of almost continuous invitations to join the faculties of other universities. As the thesis became more widely accepted and as Turner's stature and reputation as a scholar increased, the competition to secure his services intensified. One after another the major schools of the nation—Princeton, Johns Hopkins, Amherst, Chicago, California, Pennsylvania, Stanford, Harvard—offered inducements to attract the Wisconsin professor to their campuses. Turner's decision of 1910 to accept an offer from Harvard was prompted more by conditions at Madison than by the enticements offered by America's most venerable seat of learning. Nor was Harvard's offer the most generous which Turner received; a brief glance at the lures with which some institutions sought to attract this increasingly prominent historian is instructive because it indicates Turner's position within the historical fraternity and at the same time indicates that he was never guilty of seeking a new position merely for purely personal aggrandizement.

Princeton University was the first to seek Turner's services. Woodrow Wilson, himself a relatively new member of Princeton's history faculty, wrote Turner in 1896 about a chair in American history which the university's trustees had agreed to establish. The teaching load, Wilson assured Turner, would be light, and the salary would be $3,400. When this offer did not elicit a commitment from Turner, Wilson began to add other blandishments. A special fund would be provided for the purchase of American history books for the library; the proposed position would offer opportunities for lecturing which would add at least $1,500 annually to his salary; and living costs in Princeton were moderate. The insistent Wilson assured his former student that at Princeton he would be free to do his own work, and Mrs. Wilson provided a breakdown of her household expenses to indicate to the Turners that living expenses would be reasonable.[43]

Wilson's persuasions were wasted, however; after some six months of correspondence with Turner, he found himself in the embarrassing position of being forced to inform Turner that Princeton President Francis L. Patton had refused to create the chair in history, as had been promised. It seems extremely doubtful that Turner would have accepted the Princeton offer, because he felt the library facilities available at Madison were superior to those which Princeton had to offer and because of his personal attachment to Madison and to the University of Wisconsin. From this episode Turner gained experience which would be beneficial in future negotiations, and the offer improved his bargaining position with Wisconsin's regents.

Other institutions followed Princeton's lead, but none exhibited the tenacity shown by President William Rainey Harper of the University of Chicago. Harper began his campaign to bring Turner to Chicago by inviting him to teach in that school's 1898 summer term at the handsome salary of five hundred dollars for the six-week term. During the following year Turner offered a Saturday seminar at Chicago at a salary of one thousand dollars. Thus Turner became acquainted with the University of Chicago and had ample opportunity to demonstrate both his teaching ability and his personal charm. This arrangement also offered the advantage of having Turner close at hand when President Harper was ready to negotiate with him for a permanent position on the Chicago faculty.[44]

President Harper made his offer to Turner on March 10, 1900: headship of the Department of History, with a half-time teaching load and a salary of four thousand dollars for the first two years and a full-time salary of five thousand dollars thereafter. This offer was indeed a rare proposition, and Turner was understandably elated; but, since his past experience urged caution, he promised to give Harper a reply by April 1. He returned to Madison to begin bargain-

ing with the University of Wisconsin on the basis of this new offer.[45]
The requests which Turner made of the university's regents at this
time reveal clearly that his interest was in improving Wisconsin's
History Department rather than in substantially adding to his own
financial position. He asked for an additional assistant professor of
American history, enlargement of the European history staff, and
additional assistants in both American and European history; and for
himself a salary of thirty-five hundred dollars and a year's leave of
absence to do research.[46]

But President Harper had only begun his campaign. He inspired
a barrage of letters from the outstanding men on his faculty, each of
whom urged Turner to accept Harper's offer; and Harper informed
Turner that thirty thousand dollars had just become available for the
purchase of library books in American history. He added that the
annual appropriation for the purchase of history books would be
increased from five thousand to ten thousand dollars. Additional
blandishments followed: the Department of History would be expanded "to include four professors, an associate professor, four assistant professors, two instructors, and at least four assistants
. . . ."[47] A subsequent letter from Harper revealed that Chicago
was ready to offer a salary of three thousand dollars a year to entice
Turner's colleague and close friend Charles Homer Haskins from
Wisconsin to Chicago.

Armed with these additional enticements, Turner presented a
new list of requests to Wisconsin's President Charles K. Adams in
April, 1900. For himself, he added to his previous request the
services of a stenographer; but for the department his requests were
more extensive: creation of a school of history, seminar rooms in the
State Historical Society library, a new assistant professor of American history, an instructor in European history, two additional fel-
lowships, permanent appropriations for library books, and the publication of a history series in the university *Bulletin*.[48]

Somewhat surprisingly, the regents agreed to fulfill most of these
requests. A School of History was established with Turner as director, and in the following years this school attracted to Wisconsin
students from all parts of the United States who, in due course,
went to teach in universities in every section of the country. Shortly
thereafter the university lost the services of Haskins, who moved to
Harvard; but it gained by the addition of Carl Russell Fish from
Harvard and Ullrich B. Phillips from Columbia. For once, at least,
President Harper's power of persuasion met with defeat.

The success of Wisconsin's School of History made Turner more attractive to other institutions, and offers were tendered with no abatement. Following an unsuccessful attempt by Johns Hopkins to draw him away from Wisconsin, Turner in 1903 taught a six-week summer term at the University of California for the munificent salary of seven hundred fifty dollars. While in California, he renewed his acquaintance with two old friends, Max Farrand of Leland Stanford, and Henry Morse Stephens of the University of California. Each of these men was determined to attract Turner to his own school on a permanent basis, and each had the support of an energetic university president enlisted in the project.

Stanford President David Starr Jordan issued an official invitation in April, 1906, for Turner to join his faculty. He offered a salary of five thousand dollars and an annual two months' leave with pay for research. Turner was tempted by this offer, but he was concerned about the inadequacy of Stanford's library holdings. He realized that this deficiency would necessitate long periods of time away from his family while he was on research trips, and he doubted that the margin of difference between his four thousand dollar salary at Wisconsin and the five thousand dollars which Stanford was prepared to pay would be adequate to justify the move. Turner suggested, however, that he would be attracted to any university which would offer an arrangement providing for one free semester for research; such an arrangement, Turner felt, would make possible the writing and publication which could alleviate the financial worries which had become an almost permanent part of his life. Professor Farrand assured him that such an arrangement would be satisfactory with Stanford, and the University of California had already indicated that it would equal, or exceed, any offer which Stanford might make.

Turner took this information to his close friend, Charles R. Van Hise who, thanks in part to Turner, had recently been named president of the University of Wisconsin. Van Hise promised to seek private funds which would permit Turner one semester for writing each year; failing in that attempt, Van Hise would try to secure approval for such an arrangement from the regents.[49]

President Jordan's efforts to attract Turner to Stanford were fruitless. On April 17, 1906, the regents somewhat reluctantly agreed to relieve Turner of his teaching duties for one semester each year and for him to spend it in research and writing for publication.[50] Van Hise had won a victory, and Turner stayed at Wisconsin—at least

for the moment. The regents, by providing time for research and
writing, had subscribed to the principle of underwriting pure research in the humanities.

But President Van Hise's success became the instrument which
finally called for Turner's resignation. The regents, sometimes
motivated at least partially by political considerations, became increasingly hostile to the university's administration and to the plan,
previously approved by them, which gave Turner some freedom
from classes to pursue his writing. An investigation into the Van
Hise administration was launched, and Turner was required "by the
registrar's office to furnish a complete record of the time he spent in
classes, office hours, personal conferences, and examination reading. . . ."[51]

By 1909, the situation at Wisconsin had become almost intolerable for Turner, and he began to look for a new appointment. In July,
he contacted his friend Henry Morse Stephens at the University of
California, who informed him that the California offer still stood.
California's President, Benjamin I. Wheeler, hastened to arrange a
conference with Turner in Chicago on September 14, 1909. In the
meantime, Turner wrote some of his friends about the situation and
asked their advice. One of those in whom he confided was his
former student and colleague, Charles Homer Haskins, who had
moved to Harvard in 1902. Haskins received Turner's letter on the
day the latter's interview with President Wheeler was scheduled,
and Haskins sent a telegram asking that Turner delay his decision
until he could " 'see what can be done elsewhere.' "[52] Turner
agreed, and thus began the developments which resulted in Turner's
move to Harvard.

VI *Turner Moves to Harvard*

Haskins had been working for some time to arrange an offer
sufficiently attractive to Turner to bring him to Cambridge, and
now, with the knowledge that the professor had decided to leave
Wisconsin, his former pupil intensified his efforts. It was agreed
between them that Turner would not commit himself prior to October, when he was scheduled to be in Cambridge to receive an
honorary degree and to serve as an official representative of the
University of Wisconsin at the inauguration of A. Laurence Lowell
as president of Harvard.[53] Turner met with President Lowell in
Cambridge on October 5, 1909; and at that time he was offered a

newly created chair in Harvard's Department of History. The offer was, of course, subject to confirmation by the school's governing body, so Turner was not called upon for an immediate reply to the offer. On the following day, however, he wrote Mrs. Turner that he had told Haskins and President Van Hise that " 'if the election is offered I shall accept. . . .' "[54] The Harvard Corporation officially elected Turner professor of history on October 12, stipulating that he was to assume the position in the fall of 1910. His salary was to be five thousand dollars, the minimum for the professorial rank, with the promise that this would be increased to the maximum of $5,500 "soon." The Harvard Board of Overseers ratified the appointment on November 10, and it was announced in the *University Gazette* on November 12.[55]

Thus did Turner make one of the most painful decisions of his life. He submitted his resignation to President Van Hise on November 15. President Wheeler of California, when informed of the decision by Turner, expressed his disappointment but congratulated Turner; Henry Morse Stephens was already aware of the decision, for Stephens was also in Cambridge for President Lowell's inauguration. "Turner's own mood," Professor Billington states, "was one of resignation rather than jubilation, for he was conscious of the great personal sacrifice that he was making in behalf of his beloved University of Wisconsin."[56] The increasing severity of the Wisconsin regents' attacks upon the university, particularly those aimed at the College of Letters and Science, had convinced Turner that he could best serve the school and his own ideals by taking a position elsewhere. Turner clearly explained his motives for leaving in a letter to his former student and close personal friend, Carl Becker. "My attitude," he wrote,

was dictated neither by ambition nor by avarice—I need not say that to you. It was the result of a conviction that in view of certain practices and views of the influential regents here, I could do my work better, and at the same time do a service in the cause of higher education here, by going elsewhere. There was no direct attack on my position. On the contrary some of the regents with whose policy I most disagreed were friendly to me personally—and not disposed to ask for any change in my own status. But there was a general question of the place of research in the College of Letters and Science involved—hours of teaching of the men, in general, were under fire; attempts at individual regent administration were made; regent attacks in public upon the relation of the University to the school

system were being made; and a strong tendency was showing itself to
increase the technical side of our work against the cultural.[57]

The sadness which Turner experienced during the remainder of
the school year, when he permitted himself to remember that a
quarter-century of work at the University of Wisconsin was rapidly
drawing to a close, was somewhat alleviated by the flood of letters
expressing good wishes and congratulations, and by the bound volume of testimonials from former students which was presented to
him shortly before he left Madison. His current students, anxious to
take one more class with him, persuaded Turner to teach during his
last semester rather than take the leave to which he was entitled.[58]
Thus Turner's tenure at the University of Wisconsin came to an end;
after a summer vacation, he turned his attention to new tasks and
different surroundings.

VII   *Turner's Presidential Address*

In the same year that he began teaching at Harvard, Turner was
elected president of the American Historical Association. In addition to the emotional trauma and the physical problems of relocating
in Cambridge after so many years in Madison, Turner was faced
with the task of preparing his presidential address. Billington tells
us that Turner debated several topics—including "Changing American Ideals" and "Perspectives in American History"—before settling on the subject of his address.

This, the most important public speech of his career, was given
before the annual meeting of the association in Indianapolis, Indiana, on December 28, 1910. Choosing as his subject "Social Forces
in American History," Turner once again expressed his belief in the
complexity of American history and in the necessity of utilizing
information and techniques from other disciplines which could aid
in understanding the development of the American nation. "The
economist, the political scientist, the psychologist, the sociologist,
the geographer, the student of literature, of art, of religion—all the
allied laborers in the study of society—have contributions to make
to the equipment of the historian. These contributions are partly of
material, partly of tools, partly of new points of view, new hypotheses, new suggestions of relations, causes, and emphasis."[59]

Turner warned that each of these "laborers," in common with the
historian, was in "some danger of bias by his particular point of

view," but he pointed out that, in the difficult task of explaining America to Americans, the cooperation of all pertinent disciplines was essential. "If the truth is to be made known," he told this gathering of historians, "the historian must so far familiarize himself with the work and equip himself with the training of his sister-subjects that he can at least avail himself of their results and in some reasonable degree master the essential tools of their trade."[60]

Turner also returned, briefly, to a theme which always had been near the center of his thinking: the utility of restudying the past in the light of current knowledge as a means of understanding the present. To comprehend contemporary America, to gain "an understanding of the rise and progress of the forces which have made it what it was, demands that we should rework our history from the new points of view afforded by the present."[61] Turner concluded his address with a challenging statement to his colleagues, a statement expressing the expansive, all-inclusive concept of history so characteristic of him. The present duty of the American historian, Turner declared, is to "see in American society with its vast spaces, its sections equal to European nations, its geographic influences, its brief period of development, its variety of nationalities and races, its extraordinary industrial growth under the conditions of freedom, its institutions, culture, ideals, social psychology, and even its religions forming and changing almost under his eyes, one of the richest fields ever offered for the preliminary recognition and study of the forces that operate and interplay in the making of society."[62]

This address was, as Billington has pointed out, a "surprisingly modern essay," but it reiterated some of the major points which Turner had been making for many years.[63] A clear indication of Turner's "historical method," the address makes plain that he was not tied to any narrow or dogmatic interpretation of history; and it showed that his approach to an understanding of the development of modern America would range along all the academic avenues leading to additional knowledge. The essay indicated, also, that Turner practiced precisely what he urged upon his fellows: a constant reworking of history in the light of present knowledge and insight.

The pleasure which Turner must have realized from giving the presidential address to the American Historical Association was enhanced by an additional honor bestowed upon him at the Indianapolis meeting. At a dinner in his honor, hosted by his former students at the University of Wisconsin, Turner was presented a copy of *Essays in American History Dedicated to Frederick Jackson Turner*.[64] His pride in the volume was revealed in a letter to Carl Becker, whose contribution to the book Turner praised highly. He ended the letter by quoting a statement made by his friend J. Franklin Jameson: " 'You ought to be so proud of a tribute like that that it would be safest for you to carry weights in your pocket for some time'—They are there!"[65]

VIII Decline of Publications

After the publication of his presidential address, in 1911, Turner's name appeared less frequently in the *American Historical Review*. Following the appearance of the *Guide to the Study and Reading of American History* in 1912, which he coauthored with Edward Channing and Albert Bushnell Hart, Turner produced little of real consequence until the 1920s, when "Sections and Nation" (1922) and "The Significance of the Section in American History" (1925), both discussed earlier in this chapter, appeared. No books followed *Rise of the New West*; there were few essays, and even the number of book reviews diminished. Many writers, Turner included, have given thought to this decline in his published output, and a variety of possible explanations have been advanced. Turner himself, as early as 1899, recognized that he was doing painfully little writing. In that year he wrote Carl Becker that "I have not done anything, and have not the heart for anything."[66] Two of the Turners' three children had died in that year, and it has been suggested that this loss left Turner "so dispirited he never recaptured his old pace." In the same year that he accepted the Harvard position, he told a friend that his " 'craft' went tramping about to so many ports of call he could not settle to write." And he also said, probably without convincing many people, that a man over thirty has no new ideas.[67]

It can be argued, also, that Turner devoted too much of his time to his students and too little to his writing. This fact is, perhaps, what his Harvard colleague Edward Channing had in mind when he said that "Turner is a dear fellow, but he has no idea of the value of time. He has never written any big books." Edward Everett Dale, for many years head of the Department of History at the University of Oklahoma, and one of Turner's last doctoral students, recorded Channing's remark and added his own belief that writing big books was not important. "Turner could say more in one brief essay than most historians did in an entire volume."[68] Turner did spend unusual amounts of time with his students, particularly those in his seminars. Dale recalls that Turner, the most open, approachable man in the world, seemingly had unlimited time for discussing all manner of topics with his students. Students were always welcome at the Turner home, and Professor and Mrs. Turner evidently delighted in their company. Dale has recorded how cordially he was welcomed when he, forgetting the proprieties, interrupted the Turners on vacation at their seaside cottage to discuss his dissertation— a "brief" interruption that lasted a week to the evident satisfaction of all concerned.[69] Nor did Turner's interest in his students diminish when they had left the university. Turner, prolific letter writer, maintained an active correspondence with many of his former students almost until his death. He took great pride in their accomplishments, and he was quick to acknowledge an achievement with a letter of praise.[70]

One final explanation for the paucity of Turner's output remains to be considered. As we have stated elsewhere, the actual writing of a long paper was an extremely distasteful task for Turner. The sustained effort necessary to produce a book-length manuscript seems to have been physically and mentally exhausting. He suffered agonies while writing *Rise of the New West*, as has been shown previously; and the job was completed only under the insistent prodding of his editor. The challenge and the excitement of studying history, for Turner at least, was found, as we have already noted, in research—in locating the elusive fact, in uncovering additional pertinent material, in discovering a new technique, or in developing an original approach. To write what was already known when there remained areas and topics to be explored seemed to him a dreadful thing. Moreover, his doubt that all the facts had been gathered and his fear that some other discipline's viewpoint had not been considered made him reluctant to set his ideas down in writing. Realizing the extremely broad horizons embraced by Turner's concept of history, we can easily understand why he hesitated to put his thoughts and ideas into the rigid form of the printed page.

Whatever the cause—personal grief over the loss of his children, his almost total commitment to teaching, or a nature uncongenial to writing—Turner's literary output, never great, declined after he moved to Harvard. In his defense it must be noted that almost a conspiracy of events occurred which consumed much of his time and thought and which were emotionally trying. First of all, beginning in 1915, Turner—at the time secretary of the board of editors of the *American Historical Review*—was for almost two years engaged in an academic "tempest in a teapot" which threatened to split the American historical profession. For some years there had been criticism of the leadership of the American Historical Association and of the management of its publication, the *Review*. This criticism came into the open in 1913 at the association's annual meeting in Charleston, South Carolina; and the activities of a "reform" group of young historians in attendance attracted the attention of Frederic Bancroft, who soon was connected with the reform movement.

At this meeting Bancroft was elected to the association's council, and from this vantage point launched a scathing attack on the *Review's* board of editors. When Bancroft wrote a number of pamphlets which set forth his criticisms, he included charges that the board's members used the *Review* and their own influence to maintain themselves in power. He also suggested that members of the board charged to the association their costs of transportation to, and entertainment at, the annual meetings of the association. During the course of the battle, Bancroft chastised the board for maintaining "ring rule," "sophistry," and "oligarchy," and even accused them of "petty thievery."[71] Turner felt that this attack was a personal one, and he was extremely active in defending his own and the board's position. The reform movement did bring some changes in the organization of the association and in the operation of the *American Historical Review*, but the controversy was extremely unfortunate, and it left a residue of bitterness. Turner retained a large group of letters relating to this unsavory episode in sealed boxes, and the correspondence was not made public until after Turner's death.[72]

Second, Turner was increasingly troubled by developments in twentieth-century America. He had stated in his presidential address to the association that a revolution had occurred in the United States since he had presented his frontier hypothesis. He saw the nation as racked by the opposing forces of capital and labor, the native stock inundated by a flood of immigration, and the traditional political philosophy of the country threatened by the foreign ideologies of socialism and Marxism. The individual had been unable or unwilling to discipline himself; and the "unchecked development of the individual," combined with the growth of corporate power, now posed serious problems to the nation. Thus, elements of frontier democracy harbored mutual hostilities and "contained the seeds of its dissolution."[73]

He was frightened by the sheer numbers of the immigrants arriving annually, and he was alarmed by the effect these foreigners and their social and political ideologies might have upon American democracy. He noted with horror the " 'social tragedy' " of Pittsburgh, which he had earlier referred to as the pride of midwestern capitalism; for this city was now populated by "Huns, Bulgars, and Poles." His fears led him to make an uncharacteristic reference to the " 'dull-brained' Italians" who were populating the eastern cities of the United States, and to wonder whether the nation would be forced to "adjust its unique democracy to a European type."[74]

As the years passed, his own research went forward with his customary enthusiasm; and Turner gave no indication that he was dissatisfied with his situation at Harvard; and his letters indicate that he thoroughly enjoyed the "engaging young rascals" who filled his classes each term.[75] He maintained an active correspondence with his former students, now located at colleges and universities in all sections of the country; and, even after his retirement, he continued to prod students to complete their dissertations and to get articles and books published.[76] He also found time, during these Harvard years, to make a contribution to the nation's war effort with work on the National Board for Historical Service and to organize and direct the Harvard Commission on Western History, an undertaking designed to expand the Harvard Library's collections in western United States history.[77] Vacations were spent at the Turner cottage on the Maine coast or as a visiting lecturer at some school in the West.

Turner's career as a teacher ended in 1924 at the close of the academic year. His enthusiasm for research was as strong as ever; but, at sixty-three years of age, his former physical vigor was declining. The robust health of earlier years was marred now by frequent bouts with illness. The Turners had decided to spend their retirement years in Madison, the city which always had been dearest to their hearts. Their only daughter lived there, and Turner felt that in Madison he could "exist on my diminished income," which he was sure he could not do in Cambridge.[78]

However, Turner's health was adversely affected by Wisconsin's cold weather, and he decided to move to a warmer climate. After a brief stay in California, Turner was happy to accept a position as a

research associate at the Henry E. Huntington Library and Art
Gallery, a post offered Turner by his longtime friend Max Farrand,
now director of this magnificent research facility. In 1927, three
years after his retirement, the Turners moved permanently to
California.[79] The Huntington Library years, which were terminated
by Turner's death in 1932, were among Turner's happiest. During
these years Turner continued his work on sections in American
history. At the time of his death, March 14, 1932, he was working on
a volume, *The United States, 1830–1850, The Nation and Its Sections.* The manuscript for this book was edited by his friend and
former student Avery O. Craven and was published in 1935. It
garnered Turner's second Pulitzer Prize in history, his first having
been awarded in 1932 for *The Significance of Sections in American
History.*

The United States, 1830–1850 was an impressive study of the
workings of sections, and it contained an amazing amount of detailed information and statistical data; it revealed, however, no new
methods or new hypotheses. The book is uneven, and the literary
style leaves something to be desired, and it is obvious that Turner
would have further revised and polished parts of it. Since it was an
incomplete manuscript, it would be unfair to judge Turner by it.
Certain it is that Turner's "abiding faith in democracy" gleams in
this unfinished last work of one of America's outstanding historians.
We may not agree with a reviewer that "had it been finished it
undoubtedly would have been [his] masterpiece," but we would
find it difficult to take issue with the statement that the book "makes
for the completeness" of Turner's career.[80]

CHAPTER 4

Criticisms of the Frontier Thesis

JUST as awareness and acceptance of Frederick Jackson Turner's frontier thesis came slowly before it was embraced wholeheartedly by almost all members of the historical profession, so the criticism of the thesis was long in developing; indeed, the first public questioning of the thesis did not appear until the 1920s. The criticism of this decade was sporadic and tentative, and it remained that way almost until Turner's death in 1932. The passing of this great scholar seemed a signal to the critics who must have been waiting in the wings; for they suddenly sprang onto the stage in great numbers; and, sometimes with more vigor than mature thought, they launched an attack which reached its zenith in the late 1940s.

In the following decade, a "third generation" of frontier scholars moved onto the scene, men and women who were prepared to examine the thesis itself with all the modern techniques available to the serious student. This new group of social scientists found that some of the earlier, more vehement critics of Turner were themselves guilty, to a large degree, of the same errors which they assigned to Turner. The investigations of this new group served to restore, therefore, much of the validity of the thesis and to return Turner to his preeminent position among American historians. In general, a much more balanced view of the thesis has prevailed within the historical fraternity since the 1950s.

Surprisingly, the first recorded criticism of the frontier thesis was the work of Edmond S. Meany of the University of Washington, who had studied with Turner at Wisconsin. In a paper titled "The Towns of the Pacific Northwest Were Not Founded on the Fur Trade,"[1] Meany questioned a statement which Turner had written in *Rise of the New West:* "The trading posts became the nuclei of later settlement; the trader's trails grew into the early roads, and their portages marked out the location of canals. Little by little the fur trade was undermining the Indian society and paving the way for the entrance of civilization."[2] Meany recognized the soundness of this statement as applied to the settlement of lands east of the Great Divide, but Meany maintained that it did not hold true for the development of settlements in the Pacific Northwest. "It was not," Meany wrote, "the trading posts that became the towns."[3] In the Old Oregon Country, he argued, "American settlers built for themselves fresh new towns, the nuclei being usually a sawmill, a water power[site], a mine, or a convenient crossroads in the farming districts. Many of the pioneers had to build forts and stockades to protect their homes from Indians, but the dramatic life of the fur trade had vanished before the dawn of the real era of town building in Old Oregon."[4]

Professor Gene M. Gressley, who, in an excellent example of historiography, has chronicled the controversy which has enveloped the thesis, has concluded that Meany's article "made little impression on the historical profession."[5] Therefore, it was not until 1921, twelve years after the publication of Meany's dissent, that significant criticism of the thesis, or of parts of it, next appeared. The first of these attacks was launched by Charles A. Beard in a review of Turner's *The Frontier in American History,* in which Beard took issue with the frontier thesis on four points.[6]

First, Beard contended that Turner's statement that "the existence of free land, the continuous recession, [and] the advance of American settlement westward explain American development" was "too broad and sweeping." American development to 1893 was largely explained by the agrarian West, slavocracy, labor and capitalism, Beard granted, but not by the existence of free land and the westward advance of settlement alone. Second, Beard said that it "may or may not be true" that, as Turner claimed, "the frontier is the line of most rapid and effective Americanization. . . . The frontier promoted the formation of a composite nationality for the American people." This statement, Beard said, was based merely on an impression; "the data for proving it are not yet assembled. . . . There seemed to be about as much 'Americanism' among the polyglot inhabitants of New York City during the recent war as among the German and Scandinavian farmers of North Dakota."[7]

Beard's third objection was to Turner's statement that "the legislation which most developed the powers of the national government, and played the largest part in its activity was conditioned on the frontier." "The legislation in question," Beard said, "was 'influenced' but it was not 'conditioned' except in the sense in which it was also 'conditioned' by the demands and pressures of eastern capitalists and workingmen and southern planters."[8] And, fourth, Beard found little to support Turner's contention that the westward march of settlement led to an increasingly looser construction of the Constitution. "Certainly," argued Beard, "there was no period more 'loose' than that between 1789 and 1795."[9] Beard concluded his criticism by suggesting that it would be more profitable for historians to devote more attention to the conflict between labor and capital and less to the frontier hypothesis.

In the month following the publication of Beard's criticism, a second historian, Clarence Walworth Alvard, took issue with some aspects of the frontier thesis. Alvard, in a review of Turner's *The Frontier in American History*, used the opportunity to "make a few critical remarks about one of the most classical passages" in Turner's writings. The reveiwer took exception to Turner's famous and already quoted description of the migration from East to West: "Stand at Cumberland Gap and watch the procession of civilization, marching single file—the buffalo following the trail to the salt springs, the Indian, the fur-trader and hunter, the cattle-raiser, the pioneer farmer—and the frontier has passed by."[10] Alvard expressed the opinion, based upon his own studies, that the "procession of civilization" was not so nicely divided into categories as Turner's statement indicated; and he could not agree that the procession moved in such neat order, one class following another. He noted that Daniel Boone, the hunter, was accompanied by Richard Henderson, a well-educated member of the North Carolina bar; and that the first boats plying the Ohio River, "that highway to the West," carried not only fur-traders from Pennsylvania and Virginia, but prominent figures such as Thomas Walker, Christopher Gist, George Morgan, and George Washington, all of them "interested in the exploration of western lands." Alvard concluded that the various classes of men—hunters, farmers, entrepreneurs—arrived in the western country "practically simultaneously." The procession of civilization did not march single file, one wave after another: "the picture . . . of a succession of waves of immigration is incorrect. The figure should be a flood."[11]

One of the first general attacks upon the thesis appeared in 1925. In "The Shibboleth of the Frontier," Professor John C. Almack of Stanford University asserted that ". . . it does not appear that the Turner theory is in accord with the facts." Almack doubted that the frontier was primarily responsible for progressive reforms such as direct election, the improvement of civil service, or tax-supported schools. The importance which Turner assigned to the frontier in securing these improvements, Almack argued, could more accurately be assigned to labor. Noting that the frontier was not unique, Almack concluded that, while ". . . the frontier has been an important factor in American life, it has not been an important agency of progress."[12]

In the following year another Californian, John Carl Parish, presented a quite different criticism of the Turner thesis. Parish suggested that the westward movement, "in its larger sense," did not cease to exist after 1890. He agreed that the "frontier of settlement" had disappeared after 1890, as the superintendent of the census and as Turner had pointed out; but the frontier of settlement was only one of several frontiers. Historians, Parish, wrote, had been too busy "writing the obituary of a single frontier—that of settlement—that we have shut our eyes to the fact that the westward movement . . . did not cease in 1890 but has been a persistent factor in our national life. . . ." Other frontiers — conservation, in tensive farming, banking, manufacturing, the arts which Parish calls the frontiers of "material development and transforming ideas"— continued the westward movement after 1890. The "ancient spirit" of the frontier would be preserved, Parish felt, as the cultural frontier made adaptations to differing physical conditions, and as the continued strength of sectionalism was maintained.[13]

Parish's statement was the last serious criticism of the thesis presented in the 1920s. Considered collectively, this body of criticism, which had begun with Meany's article in 1909, had been somewhat ill defined; certainly, it had not been devastating. In comparison with the attacks which the following two decades brought, the criticisms of the 1920s seem almost innocuous. A deluge of criticism of the frontier thesis and of Turner himself, some of it extremely vitriolic, began in 1930 and continued for two decades. At least two factors help to explain the volume and the severity of this criticism of the frontier thesis and its author in the 1930s and 1940s.

I Reasons for Increased Criticism

In the first place, a wave of criticism would be a natural reaction to the years during which the thesis had been the recipient of enthusiastic and nearly total acceptance. Turner's students, in the years following the enunciation of the thesis, had spread throughout the United States; and scarcely a major school in the country did not include at least one representative of Wisconsin's School of History. Moreover, these young scholars, who were more often than not imbued with the zeal of disciples, believed fervently that they were academic missionaries ordained to spread the new gospel of the significance of the frontier. As is often the case with disciples, these men were sometimes led by their fervor to make claims much more extravagant than those the master himself would have advanced. Turner was a cautious scholar, and he was aware that he had outlined an hypothesis whose value would be known only after rigorous testing. His followers often held no such reservations; to them, as Billington has noted, "the thesis was the Divine Word, utterly unassailable."[14] And the disciples did not labor in vain; for, by the 1920s, as one critic of the thesis noted, the American Historical Association had become " 'One Big Turner *Verein.*' "[15]

Nor was this worship of the Turner hypothesis confined to the followers of Clio. Scholars in the areas of economics, political science, and geography were entranced by the frontier concept; and studies were undertaken in all these areas to reinterpret earlier conclusions in light of the Turner hypothesis. In the field of literature, the acceptance of the thesis precipitated a flood of books which considered the role of the midwestern frontier and the prairie in the making of America and in the development of American literature.[16] Nor did the political arena escape the pervasive influence of the frontier thesis. Governor Philip La Follette of Wisconsin used the thesis as the basis for an appeal for authority to expand the social services provided by his state government.[17] Both President Franklin D. Roosevelt and his opponents used the thesis as they debated methods to deal with the problems of unemployment during the Depression. And, in considering American foreign policy, both imperialists and anti-imperialists made reference to the thesis as a partial justification of their respective positions.[18] The cumulative effect of so much attention to the thesis, and of such uncritical acceptance of it, made a critical reaction to it virtually inevitable.

In the second place, the intellectual atmosphere engendered by the economic catastrophe which began in 1929 demanded a critical reappraisal of this thesis which centered upon a less complex and nonindustrialized age. A new generation of historians, who reached their professional majority during the Depression decade, ". . . re-

belled against emphasis on rural past when the problems that demanded solution stemmed from an urban present."[19] To such men,
Billington has written, "an interpretation of the American past that
stressed agrarianism rather than industrialism, rugged individualism rather than state planning, and optimistic nationalism
rather than political internationalism seemed outmoded. . . .
Younger scholars . . . were ready to rebel against over-glorification
of the useless agrarian past, ready to demand a reinterpretation in
terms of a usable recent past that would help them understand the
complexities of an urban culture at a time when civilization seemed
out of joint."[20]

Thus, the decade of the 1930s witnessed an outpouring of criticism, the volume and rancor of which caused the attacks of the
previous decade to pale in comparison. Benjamin F. Wright, a professor of government at Harvard University, opened the attack of
the Depression decade. In the first of several articles and reviews
dealing with Turner and his thesis, Wright questioned the role of
the frontier in the development of democracy. He expressed the
belief that Turner had erred in his "tendency to separate the growth
of American democracy from the general course of Western Civilization." Wright doubted that democracy came from the American
forest; it was more probable, he thought, that democracy moved
across the continent from the East and became stronger in the
West, where conditions were conducive to its growth.[21]

Wright also contended, on the basis of his own research, that the
frontiersman was not the unique, creative individual Turner had
supposed him to be; he was, Wright maintained, an imitative rather
than an originative individual, as evidenced by the constitutions
frontiersmen wrote for their new western states. Finally, Wright
called for a better definition of frontier than Turner had given —
one that would give more adequate consideration to factors other
than geography.[22]

In the first year of Franklin D. Roosevelt's first administration,
Professor Louis Hacker criticized the thesis from a Marxian viewpoint. Turner's "uniqueness of the frontier experience and the con-
tinuity of sectional differences" were dismissed by Hacker in a
cavalier manner. In agreement with Professor Wright, Hacker believed that excessive emphasis of the frontier experience and of
sectional development had introverted American historiography
when "all eyes should have been on events going on beyond the

country's borders." Hacker expressed acceptance of the safety-valve theory of the frontier, but he pointed out that, by luring factory workers to free farm lands in the West, the American labor movement was deprived of a continuous revolutionary tradition.[23]

Charles A. Beard took up his charges again in the closing year of the decade. He was still perplexed by the Turnerians' neglect of the "democratic impulses in Eastern idealism" of the labor movement, and he was convinced that the frontier exhibited characteristics of cooperation as well as individualism. Beard doubted that the frontier exerted as much influence as Turnerians claimed for it, but he expressed an interest in determining what kind of influence it had had and the extent of it.[24]

Scholars during the 1930s directed a great deal of research toward various aspects of the frontier thesis; and, partly because of the dismal employment conditions which prevailed in that decade, much attention was devoted to the safety-valve theory. This theory was not an integral part of the Turner thesis, as Gressley has stated, but the two have long been associated.[25] As a matter of fact, Turner did not emphasize the safety-valve theory in his writings and he did not insist on the theory even though he, like de Tocqueville, recognized its importance. But, as Professor George W. Pierson once observed, "it may . . . prove hard for the frontier school to surrender the notion."[26] In the 1930s, the safety-valve theory received the unflattering attention of a bevy of economic historians.

Professors Carter Goodrich and Sol Davison of Columbia University initiated the attack on the safety-valve theory. Finding the manuscript census records of the General Land Office inadequate to their purposes, Goodrich and Davison undertook a study of westward migration based primarily on information taken from contemporary newspapers. On the basis of the availability of such sources, they began their study with migration from Fall River, Massachusetts; and they later included Lowell and Springfield, Massachusetts, in their study. They found that, although many workers left Fall River for the West, seven out of ten eventually returned to the East. They discovered, too, that the greatest deterrent to westward migration was the cost involved. Despite attempts to reduce such costs by group-migration ventures, and the occasional support of philanthropy, lack of capital kept the number of migrants relatively small. Eastern industrial wage earners reaching the frontier, concluded Goodrich and Davison, were too few to attract attention there; and their flight had little effect upon labor conditions in the East.[27]

In their study of the wage earner in the westward movement, Goodrich and Davison found no reason to question the doctrine that the presence of the frontier had slowed the industrialization of America; and they found that many potential wage earners, as distinguished from those already a part of the industrial labor force, did swell the ranks of the westward movement, thereby indicating that there was a safety valve in the frontier, but one which operated primarily for the farmer rather than for the industrial wage earner.[28]

The attack upon the safety-valve theory launched by Goodrich and Davison was joined by other historians. Three months after the Goodrich-Davison article, Professor Fred A. Shannon presented the results of his study of the effects of the Homestead Act upon western settlement. Shannon, who devoted much of his life to research and writing about the American farmer, concluded that the Homestead Act was of no help in settling the immigrant in the West. Also, Shannon's research convinced him that, of what movement occurred, it was from one farm to another more westerly farm and from farm to city; he found little evidence of movement from city to farm. Moreover, Shannon pointed out that, while the traditional frontier may have ended in 1890, as Turner stated, the West was not fully settled at that time but was just beginning to fill up.[29]

Professor Murray Kane joined the ranks of critics of the safety-valve theory in 1936. From a study of selected counties in Massachusetts and Michigan, Kane found that a small number of industrial workers returned, in periods of depression, to the agricultural communities from which they had come; rarely, however, did those workers move to free lands along the frontier.[30] As a matter of fact, the holding power of urban areas traditionally had been great, and financial considerations usually made it impossible for the unemployed industrial worker to move from the city of his unemployment.

These attacks upon the safety-valve theory and upon Turner's hypothesis did not long go unanswered. Joseph Schafer, who had been one of Turner's students, quickly rose to his teacher's defense. In December, 1936, in the first of three articles in reply to the criticisms directed at the frontier concept, Schafer took Goodrich and Davison to task for their methodology; and he stressed the psychological effect which the frontier had exerted on the development of the United States.[31]

Schafer's articles called forth a reply from Goodrich and Davison. In this reply the Columbia professors pointed out that they were interested in migration from the eastern United States, not in migration from Europe; and they maintained their position concerning the use of the manuscript census records. They accepted Schafer's argument that the possibility of moving to free land on the frontier exerted an influence on national development, but they pointed out that the effect of the existence of such free land was not measurable.[32]

In 1945, Fred A. Shannon published an article which he hoped would close debate on what he termed the "safety-valve myth." Shannon's research indicated that for every industrial worker who went into agriculture there were twenty farmers who moved to urban areas, and that for each son of a farmer who became the owner of a new farm there were ten sons who went to the city. As to immigrants, Professor Shannon doubted that many of them, after a brief stay in the factories, moved to western lands. Most of them, he felt, stayed in the industrial area where they had first settled, thereby serving to depress the labor situation. Furthermore, Shannon pointed out that strikes and associated violence reached alarming proportions in the 1870s and 1880s—the decades in which the safety valve should have been working most effectively. He suggested that had the safety valve been working, drawing off surplus factory workers, wages might have been maintained at a level high enough to prevent the great wave of strikes.[33]

Shannon's desire to lay to rest the debate on the safety-valve theory was not realized. The debate flared with renewed vigor at the fifty-first annual meeting of the Mississippi Valley Historical Association in Minneapolis, Minnesota in April, 1958; for Professor Norman J. Simler, who opened the discussion at that meeting, presented a paper in which he reviewed the criticisms of the safety-valve theory which had been made by Goodrich and Davison, Shannon, and Kane. He felt that the evidence produced by Goodrich and Davison did not constitute "a valid derogatory criticism of an economic safety-valve, whatever it may imply for an actual physical specimen of one."[34] Simler also conteneded that Goodrich and Davison had concerned themselves not with the broad question of whether the safety-valve worked at all, but with the "economically irrelevant" question of how well it worked.[35]

Simler was particularly critical of the interpretation which Shannon had placed upon the statistics of population growth and movement. He condemned Shannon, along with other critics and with defenders of the safety-valve concept, for having "been bewitched by the belief that Easterners had to become Western farmers in order for favorable effects in the Eastern labor market to occur," and he stated that "Shannon reduced this to an absurdity by making it appear necessary that the increase in owner-occupied farms in the West was the relevant variable."[36]

Turning to Murray Kane's criticism, Professor Simler stated that Kane was guilty of narrowing the issue even more than Shannon had done. Whereas Shannon was concerned with eastern wage earners becoming western farmers, Kane was concerned with eastern wage earners who became western farmers in times of panic or depression. Simler also took issue with Kane's insistence that, "in order for the safety-valve doctrine to win out, . . . many" or a majority of these workers must migrate to the West. Simler argued that it was not necessary for large numbers of wage earners to "leave a labor market in order to relieve downward pressure on wage and employment."[37] All in all, Professor Simler agreed with the critics of the social safety valve who maintained that the West had offered little escape for the eastern wage earner; he maintained, however, that there had operated an economic safety valve. "After all," Simler told the historians assembled in Minneapolis, "the West . . . did get populated and it clearly did not get that way by a process of 'spontaneous generation.' "[38]

Simler's paper, when it appeared in *Agricultural History*, was followed by a statement from Fred A. Shannon. Anyone attempting to revive the safety-valve theory, Professor Shannon wrote, "should use something more potent than legerdemain and economic jargon." Shannon pointed out that a safety valve should "prevent explosion, and explosions occurred. Therefore, the safety-valve was a mere theory and not an actuality."[39]

Yet another historian, Thomas P. Abernethy of the University of Virginia, brought to a close the criticisms of the 1930s. Professor Abernethy centered his attention upon the role of the frontier in American development. He denied that it had fostered democracy; it had, he contended, given rise to aristocracy, crudity, and opportunism. As Abernethy saw it, the figure looming large on the frontier was not Turner's sturdy, independent "hewer," but the land-speculator-politician.[40]

II *Criticism of the 1940s and 1950s*

The criticism of Turner and the frontier thesis exhibited two characteristics in the 1940s and 1950s: the attacks were more moderate in tone, and some of the critics offered alternatives to the frontier thesis. Arthur M. Schlesinger, Sr., an advocate of urban history, presented the first criticism of the thesis in the 1940s, and he pointed fellow historians in a new direction. Professor Schlesinger argued that it was time for a reinterpretation of American history—an interpretation which would recognize the rapid growth of urban areas and the role which cities had played in the development of the nation. Schlesinger pointed out that as early as 1820 migration to the cities was more rapid than migration to the frontier; by 1860, one out of every six persons in the United States was living in a town or city whose population was eight thousand or more; and, in the century from 1790 to 1890, the urban population growth was 139-fold as compared to the overall national population growth of 16-fold.

One of the important results of this rapid urban growth, Schlesinger noted, was a cultural lag between city and rural dwellers which indicated the divergent ways of life which had developed in the United States. It was Schlesinger's belief that the 1890 census director's statement actually was the announcement of a new era of American life rather than the death-knell for an old era. Schlesinger indicated, moreover, that Turner himself, as early as 1925, had anticipated an urban reinterpretation of American history.[41]

Following closely the publication of Schlesinger's criticism, Professor Murray Kane returned to the scene. Kane felt that Turner had both misused and overused anthropological and geographical factors. According to Kane, Turner's theories become a "statistical interpretation of history rather than a historical interpretation of statistics."[42] Kane felt that Turner had been correct in stressing economic factors, but he concluded that Turner had used the terminology of the economist rather than that of the geographer.[43]

An indefatigable critic of the Turner thesis, George W. Pierson, launched in the fall of 1940 the first of several articles attacking the thesis. In this elaborate and wide-ranging criticism—it included a questionnaire designed to poll historians on their attitude toward the thesis and criticisms of it—Pierson found much that disturbed him. Pierson recognized that the frontier presented unusual problems, but he assigned much of the frontier's influence to repetition, thus echoing earlier criticism that the frontier was not innovative. In common with other critics, Pierson was perplexed by the impreciseness of Turner's definition and use of such words as "democracy" and "frontier." Turner's frontier, Pierson wrote, "was hazy and a shifting concept, riddled with internal contradictions, overlaid with sectional bias, and saturated with nationalistic emotion."[44]

In 1945, the Turner thesis was attacked from a no less exalted position than the presidency of the American Historical Association. In his presidential address, Carlton J. H. Hayes, a professor of European history, deplored what he saw as the obsession of Americans with sectional and local history. Such an attitude, the American Historical Association president said, led to self-centeredness and isolation. This chauvinistic attitude was "unrealistic, contrary to the basic historical facts, and highly dangerous for our country at the present and in the future." He urged American historians in particular, and American citizens in general, to develop a broader understanding of Europe.[45]

The following year Professor James C. Malin criticized Turner for what Malin called his "peculiar absorption" with the closed-space concept. In several articles which appeared in the 1940s, Malin expressed his belief that, if mobility were essential for individual opportunity, there was little cause to be concerned about a substitute for the frontier; for, so long as the communication revolution continued, mobility in space was possible.[46]

Debate on the thesis reached its peak in the 1940s, and criticism of the thesis waned in the 1950s. This transitional period was bridged by the penetrating observations of two outstanding historians, Henry Nash Smith and Richard Hofstadter. In their writings in the late 1940s and the 1950s, they focused attention upon what they termed the "agrarian myth."

III *The Agrarian Myth*

In *Virgin Land* (1950), Professor Smith took notice of what appeared to him to be an inconsistency in Turner's theory. Smith found Turner saying, at one point, that the highest social values were to be found in "the relatively primitive society just within the agricultural frontier" and, at another point, that society evolved through several stages into an industrial civilization. Professor Smith felt that Turner was unable to make a definite choice between these two statements. Smith also condemned the popular images of the frontier for having nourished an agrarian myth which caused Americans to ignore the industrial revolution altogether, "or to regard it as an unfortunate and anomalous violation of the natural order of things." This provincial attitude, Smith argued, "tended to divert attention from the problems created by industrialization for a half century during which the United States has become the most powerful industrial nation in the world."

Moreover, Smith said, this agrarian myth affected politics and foreign affairs. "Distrust of the city . . . has impeded cooperation between farmers and factory workers in more than one crisis of our history, . . . and the agrarian myth has made it difficult for Americans to think of themselves as members of a world community because it has affirmed that the destiny of this country leads her away from Europe toward the agricultural interior of the continent." But, Professor Smith concluded, the great difficulty of the agrarian tradition is "that it accepted the paired but contradictory ideas of nature and civilization as a general principle of historical and social interpretation. A new intellectual system was requisite before the West could be adequately dealt with in literature or its social development fully understood."[47]

Richard Hofstadter also considered the agrarian myth. Hofstadter, in an article which appeared in 1948, summarized previous criticisms which had been directed at Turner's frontier thesis and added his own keen observations about the thesis.[48] Hofstadter found that the success of commercial agriculture had destroyed the agrarian myth. The idealism of Thomas Jefferson's sturdy yeoman farmer, which had existed mostly in the minds of nonfarmers or of substantial planters, gave way to the more realistic view of the actual tiller of the soil whose attachment to the land was the result not of some mystical earth-force but of a highly developed profit motive. The availability of vast amounts of public land kindled the spirit of gambling for fast profit, but it did little to strengthen the desire to become the owner of a farm in fee simple. The significance of self-sufficiency for the early western farmer, Hofstadter noted a little later, was that self-sufficiency enabled him to realize great profit.[49]

Professor Hofstadter concluded his 1949 articles by condemning Turner for failing to see the full importance of the fact that the United States not only had a frontier but that it was, itself, a frontier—"a major outlet for the countries of Western Europe during the nineteenth century." He argued that since Europe shared—through millions of its citizens who immigrated to the United States—to such an extent in the economic safety-valve aspect of the frontier, then surely the uniqueness of the frontier "must be considerably modified."[50]

IV   *The Criticisms in Support of Turner*

So ran the major criticisms of Turner and his thesis from the 1920s into the 1950s. In summary, some critics complained that Turner's terminology was hazy, that his theory was shot through with contradictions, and that his methodology was loose and poorly constructed. Other historians, with more solid evidence, pointed out that Turner had overstressed the frontier as an explanation of American development; that the thesis did not take into account such an obviously significant occurrence in American history as industrialization; and that, by directing the attention of Americans inland, westward across the continent, the thesis had made it difficult for them to accept the burgeoning role of the United States in world affairs. Still others noted that Turner did not give sufficient weight to the role of the land speculator and the prevalence of the profit motive in frontier society. It was maintained by other critics that the frontier did not give birth to democracy, that this concept was conceived elsewhere—in Europe and along the Atlantic coast of the United States—and found on the frontier a congenial environment for its maturation.

Some of these criticisms were mere exercises in nitpicking; or worse, they were attempts to gain reputation by belittling the work of others. Some of the criticisms more properly could have been directed at his disciples rather than toward Turner himself. But some of the criticisms were valid; they raised provocative questions which brought forth well-reasoned replies from students of frontier history. Even more important, perhaps, criticism of the thesis sometimes resulted in the formulation of new hypotheses or in refreshing reappraisals of the nation's past. In almost every instance, criticism stirred defenders to action.

The early attacks on the Turner thesis occasioned no immediate replies; but Frederic L. Paxson, an outstanding man of the frontier school, was among the first to use Turner's thesis in his own writing. Although Paxson cannot be considered a defender of the frontier thesis, at least on the basis of his major writings, he did recognize the significance of the thesis. "The influence of the frontier," he observed in *The Last American Frontier*—his study of the westward movement from the Mississippi—"has been the strongest single factor in American history. . . . [51] Writing fourteen years later, however, Paxson revealed some reservations about the thesis. "The first century of American independence was dominated by the influence of the frontier," he stated; but he added that "its second seems likely to be shaped by industry and pressure of the outside world."[52]

Carl Becker, who had studied under Turner at the University of Wisconsin, made the first specific reply to critics of the frontier thesis in 1927.[53] In a beautifully written tribute to his former teacher, Becker enumerated traits which would be repeated by other defenders of Turner and his thesis. Turner's approach was, Becker believed, to understand institutions rather than to judge them. Becker was concerned lest Turner's descriptive style hide the fact that his thesis was the result of exhaustive research; and he made it clear that Turner's bias, if he had any, was Americanism. "Turner's fame must rest," Becker wrote, "not upon the massed bulk of books published, but upon the virtue and vitality of the ideas he has freely scattered about. . . . This is enough; and this, I think, must be accorded to Turner."[54]

Professor Merle Curti, also a former Turner student, entered the ranks of Turner defenders in 1931. In an essay concerning Turner's methodological concepts, Curti noted, as Becker had, the absence of dogmatism in Turner's work. Turner wrote, Curti said, "as though his wiser successor would correct, reconstruct, and be reconstructed." Curti reminded those critics who felt that Turner had not given industrial development sufficient prominence in his thesis that Turner was concerned primarily with the United States during its agricultural period. Moreover, at the time Turner presented his thesis in 1893, industrialization was just reaching substantially large areas of the nation; therefore, its effect upon American democracy could not have been adequately considered at that time. In his presidential address to the American Historical Association in 1910, Curti observed that Turner did indicate the importance of industrial capitalism in the development of the United States.[55]

Joseph Schafer began a defense of his former teacher shortly after Turner's death in 1932. In articles which appeared in *Wisconsin Magazine of History*, Schafer reiterated the characteristics of Turner's work which Becker and Curti had earlier advanced. Schafer wanted it understood that Turner did not consider western expansion as the sole explanation of American development, but rather that he viewed it as the most important single key to an understanding of American history.[56] Schafer continued his defense of Turner; and, as editor of the *Wisconsin Magazine of History*, he succeeded in turning that journal into "a vehicle dedicated to honoring the memory of Turner."[57]

Avery O. Craven, a prolific writer and one of the most influential of Turner's students, began in 1937 a series of articles which supported the frontier thesis. Professor Craven maintained that the exposure of institutions to free land was an experience unique to the United States—a position which some Turner critics, notably Louis Hacker, had denied.[58] Furthermore, to subjugate the agricultural interpretation of American history to the industrial perspective would be to deny the effect of two hundred years of agricultural dominance.[59]

Craven admitted that critics were correct in seeing contradictions and exceedingly broad generalizations in Turner's work. It was impossible to remove all contradictions, Craven said, because those "who knew the man and his work at first hand were seldom conscious of contradictions."[60] As to generalizations, Craven said that Turner abhorred generalizations; but the type of history which he wrote required generalizations. Turner's emphasis was on the general, rather than the specific, character of change.[61]

In another essay Professor Craven discussed the breadth and unity of Turner's historical concepts, and he indicated the significant influence which Turner had had upon American historiography. He touched upon the philosophical aspects of Turner's work and concluded that his teacher had possessed the "ability to see deep into the meaning of things and [the] power to catch the universals."[62] Craven subsequently modified some of his views on Turner. "In the light of present day scholarship," Craven wrote in 1951, "it seems quite apparent that Turner overstressed the comparative influence of the frontier in producing both nationalism and democracy. Other forces certainly had a hand in this. He recognized but he did not always properly evaluate the contradictions inherent in his approach. The West was both national and provincial in its temper; it was both materialistic and idealistic; it was both radical and conservative; it was both individualistic and cooperative. Turner also applied his findings to the Old West and he lent his findings to other wests where they won't work."[63]

By the middle of the twentieth century, interest in the frontier thesis found a different form of expression—the thesis was to be applied and tested with all the techniques now available to social science. In 1949, Ray A. Billington and James B. Hedges presented *Westward Expansion,* a volume which encompassed the story of American expansion westward from first settlement until 1896.[64] In his preface Billington stated that the book attempted "to follow the pattern that Frederick Jackson Turner might have used had he ever compressed his voluminous research on the American frontier within one volume." The outline he had used for the book, Billington continued, was "roughly that prepared by Professor Turner for his course on the history of the frontier at Harvard University."[65] The success of this application of the thesis was soon verified by the acceptance which *Westward Expansion* received. The volume has become a classic in its field; it is valued for its masterful treatment of its subject and for its excellent bibliography.[66]

Walter Prescott Webb applied the frontier thesis on a much larger scale in *The Great Frontier.*[67] Webb was convinced that the Great Frontier was diminishing rapidly in the twentieth century. Looking toward the future, he saw a tendency toward stronger governments more frequently employing compulsion; a move toward socialism (as in Great Britain and the United States) or absolutism (as in Fascist states and Communist Russia); and the loss of individual identity within the growing corporate state.[68]

John D. Barnhart made a different test of the Turner interpretation in his *Valley of Democracy,* which was published in 1953. Barnhart applied the frontier interpretation to a specific time and place: the Ohio Valley during the years 1775–1818.[69] Barnhart's study convinced him that his results paralleled Turner's interpretation; the early settlers in the Ohio Valley had made significant contributions to the development of democracy in the United States. A year after Barnhart's book appeared two University of Chicago professors, Stanley Elkins and Eric McKitrick, devised another test for the frontier thesis. Feeling, as Turner had, that there was an organic connection between American democracy and the American frontier, they sought to test this belief in a conceptual framework. Robert K. Merton had demonstrated, from careful studies of public-housing communities, that, when new settlements immediately faced staggering fundamental problems, they were forced into citizen participation in government. Thus, modern experience indicated that democracy was a natural response to problems faced by new settlements not yet equipped with adequate governmental structure.[70] Elkins and McKitrick decided to apply Merton's theory of political democracy as a test of Turner's belief concerning the relationship between American democracy and the American frontier. These historians studied new communities on three American frontiers—the Old Northwest, the Old Southwest, and Massachusetts Bay—and determined that

we may safely award Frederick Jackson Turner his due. His insight may indeed have been crude in form, but, crude as it was, for sixty years it has remained in many ways the closest thing that we have had to a seminal contribution to the theory of American history.

Yet Turner, after all, has been pre-empting the frontier long past his time. It should no longer be necessary to force literal meaning from his texts, now that they have entered our cultural metaphor. At the same time a host of problems may be examined with fresh interest if we put in testable terms facts which he knew by instinct: the fact that the experience forced by the frontier was unique—that in a century of westward expansion it was repeated over and over, that in a multitude of forms it found its way into the daily habits of the people, making Americans truly and profoundly different from anyone else in the world.[71]

This study, made more than half a century after Turner stated his thesis, reaffirmed a point which Turner had made persistently: that at least a part of the uniqueness of the American character was attributable to the repeated process of "beginning over again" on each succeeding frontier.

Another careful and scientific test of Turner's belief that American democracy developed in frontier communities was made by Professor Merle Curti. Curti selected Trempealeau County, Wisconsin, primarily because of the availability of records essential to his purpose. His plan, as he outlined it to the Newberry Conference on American Studies, was to study an actual frontier and see what the records and other evidence still at hand did show about democratic practices on that frontier—about individualism, widespread participation in the making of decisions about the common life, and equality of economic and cultural opportunity. As far as we know, no one has yet examined microscopically a given area that experienced transition from wilderness to a settled community with the purpose of determining how much democracy, in Turner's sense, did exist initially; in the first phase of settlement during the process of settlement itself, and in the period following settlement.[72]

This exhaustive study of Trempealeau County led Professor Curti and his associates to the conclusion that, while the Turner thesis needed some qualification and revision, its basic aspects withstood the test to which they had submitted it. "Our study," Curti wrote, "lends support to what we believe are the main implications of Turner's thesis about the frontier and democracy, so far as Trempealeau County is concerned." Their study, Curti concluded, indicated that "Turner's poetical vision of free land and of relatively equal opportunity was for a great many people being realized in Trempealeau County. The story of the making of this American community is a story of progress toward democracy."[73]

In the late 1950s and in the decade of the 1960s, the Turner thesis was applied to the developmental processes of nations other than the United States. Peter J. Coleman, studying the applicability of the frontier thesis to New Zealand, found that "the frontier concept provides an inadequate explanation for the kind of society that emerged in New Zealand." Coleman pointed out, however, that he did not contend "that the frontier was without its influence. . . ."[74] In the past decade, other scholars in several academic disciplines have undertaken comparative studies of frontiers in a number of countries. These attempts to apply the frontier thesis generally have been less than conclusive, perhaps because the thesis has not been applied as systematically as it might have been.[75]

Also, in the 1960s, as popular interest in the history of the Negro quickened, Turner's writing was reviewed in order to learn how he had dealt with slavery as a factor in the frontier advance.[76] Staughton Lynd has argued that slavery was a troublesome factor which Turner could not fit into his thesis and that, reflecting his own time, he shifted attention from slavery to the frontier. Lynd also contends that both Turner and Beard "systematically minimized" the significance of slavery.[77]

Thus, in the forty years since Turner's death, his frontier thesis has been both attacked and defended with vigor; it has been tested and evaluated by all the methods available to social scientists; and it has been applied to frontier situations outside the United States. As for the effect upon the standing of his frontier thesis at the present time, the most obvious answer is that few historians today either accept the thesis in its totality or reject it completely; neither the attitude of Joseph Schafer nor that of George W. Pierson would hold sway in the 1970s. Most historians recognize that there is much of value in the thesis, but they are also aware that it possesses some serious limitations. They generally agree that the thesis is not the only key to an understanding of this country's development, and they realize that Turner never suggested that it was.

No other thesis has had as much impact upon the teaching and the study of United States history as has the frontier thesis, and this thesis is doing today what it has been doing for almost eighty years: it is stimulating the current generation of historians to probe more deeply into all the theories of American development. Professor Roy F. Nichols recognized this fact when he addressed a meeting of the European Association for American Studies in Paris in 1957. "Historians and social scientists," he told the group, "are . . . studying the implications of the mobility of American population and its influence upon American national character and democracy. . . . Undoubtedly a more realistic and comprehensive theory of American cultural development will be formulated by some new Turner, who may be a committee. It will be more complex but it may well still be concerned primarily with migration. This new theory will probably still be based on the great factor of population movement but it will not be simply westward movement but complex movement in all directions."[78]

CHAPTER 5

Turner and American Historiography

FREDERICK Jackson Turner exerted a profound impact upon American historiography as both a writer and a teacher. The effects of his work were evident in his own lifetime, and his interpretations of United States history have been accepted by succeeding generations of scholars as classic approaches to an understanding of the American past. As a writer and as a teacher, Turner made outstanding contributions and achieved lasting influence; and both roles must be considered in order to obtain an accurate picture of Turner the historian. Over the years it has become traditional to think of Turner as a writer rather than as a teacher; therefore, it may be well to look first at his written contributions to the field of history.

I Turner as Scholar and Writer

His essays reveal Turner to have been a sound and meticulous scholar whose interests ranged over a broad spectrum of man's activities. He was confined to no particular philosophy of history, nor to any single time or place in the past. He resented the label "western historian"; for, as a man well trained in late nineteenth-century historical concepts, he was perfectly at ease with European history, a subject which he taught for many years. Nor did he believe that the historian was confined, in his study, to the area and methodology of history. He used, and encouraged his "seminarians" to use, the tools and techniques of other social sciences; and he argued that the good historian must also be a geographer, a political scientist, a sociologist, a geologist, an economist. "I have been interested," he said in 1925, "in the inter-relations of economics, politics, sociology, culture in general, with the geographic factors, in explaining the United States today by means of its history thus broadly taken."[1]

Because Turner sought the meaning of man's past actions in many and various disciplines, he recognized that there could be no simple explanation, no single key, to unlock the mysteries of history. He rejected as incomplete such current "keys to history" as the struggles between Puritan and cavalier, slavery and freedom, state and nation, and capital and labor. "In truth," he said in 1907, "there is no single key to American history. In history, as in science, we are learning that a complex result is the outcome. Simple explanations fail to meet the case."[2] Turner is revealed, therefore, as a multiple causationist; he could not explain history solely in terms of either frontier or section, nor in terms of the various "struggles" with which some of his colleagues sought simple answers. His study of causes and forces in many fields which, in various combinations, affected the activities of man led Turner to accept the principle of relativism sooner than most scholars.

But Turner recognized another aspect of relativism. History, he thought, must be relevant to the present. Therefore, history could never be static; explanations could never be complete or final; and the best the historian could hope for would be to reach a sound, *tentative*, conclusion. The next generation of scholars would take this tentative conclusion, evaluate it in the light of additional knowledge, and modify it for the new present. "Each age," Turner once stated, "writes the history of the past anew with reference to conditions upper-most in its own time." Thus Turner pointed out the obligation of historians to write usable history—history which spoke of the past in terms possessed of meaning in the present.

This admonition to write history was bitter medicine for Turner. He was never really ready to write and when, under the pressure of deadlines, he did so, it was a trying ordeal. He wrote by virtue of necessity, as Wilbur Jacobs has noted; and no one was more acutely aware of his own limitations as a writer than was Turner. He acknowledged that he had difficulty in handling the "narrative side" of writing, especially when the narrative had to be in condensed form. His strength, he believed, was in "interpretation, correlation, elucidation of large tendencies to bring out new points of view, and in giving a new setting." He was concerned with amassing evidence, collecting statistics, and correlating facts from various adademic disciplines. Such a desire to deal with all aspects and ramifications of a subject made it extremely difficult for Turner to begin writing at all, and it made the development of a good prose style well-nigh impossible.

The vast scope of Turner's investigations was another deterrent to his writing. His concept of history was complex and all-inclusive; for him there were no simple explanations of the nation's past—no brief, glittering phrases which adequately summed up United States history. For Turner, the all-inclusive scope of history had to be painted with bold strokes on a gigantic canvas, with every character and event carefully depicted and evaluated, and each arranged in proper perspective. Indeed, proper perspective, or historical proportion, was a constant problem for Turner. He likened historical writing to describing a large animal, an elephant, for example. Lack of perspective and outright omissions were worse faults than inaccurate statements, Turner maintained. "If I aim to describe an elephant, and give only an account of his feet, alleging at the same time that this constitutes the elephant, the microscopic accuracy and keenness of criticism of these organs will not atone for the failure to speak to the rest of the animal." Turner realized that "the whole dynamic body of American history" must not be lost in a welter of static detail.[3]

Perhaps the combination of vast topical scope and minute examination of detail in a literary form brief enough to be practical is an impossibility; without question, such a requirement posed severe problems for Turner. It helps explain the relatively small number of books which Turner wrote and it goes far in explaining his preference for the essay form in which he could either examine a single fact microscopically or sketch boldly some original idea without the necessity of explaining its every aspect. Clearly Turner lacked the natural ability of a Francis Parkman or a William Prescott, as Wilbur Jacobs has commented; and his style, which often employed the colorful imagery and broad, sweeping phrases of the public speaker, sometimes hinted of his early training as an orator. His style was adequate, nevertheless, to express brilliant concepts and interpretations which revitalized the study of American history.

Turner made further valuable contributions to historiography when he suggested new directions in the pursuit of historical understanding and new topics for historical investigation. United States history, Turner argued, could be understood only in its relationship to world history. Furthermore, he suggested that a study of America's impact upon Europe might be as rewarding as had been historians' concern with Europe's impact upon America. He offered an enticing list of areas for investigation—capital growth, immigration, industrialization, physiography, cultural development—and he himself planned a thorough study of the process of urbanization and its effects upon the nation. Turner believed that a thorough knowledge of these and many other topics related to United States history was essential to the "total understanding of the past."[4]

But it was not these wide-ranging contributions to historiography, nor his obvious scholarship, upon which Turner's reputation as an outstanding interpreter of American history was based. That reputation, as Howard R. Lamar has written, rested "squarely on the fame of his 'frontier thesis.' . . ."[5] In Turner's short essay—Samuel E. Morison called it "the most influential ever written on American history"—Turner presented a thesis which demanded a reappraisal of American history, a process of revision which continues to the present time.[6] The frontier hypothesis was followed by a second seminal idea, the role of the geographic section in the development of the United States. This concept also received widespread attention among historians; and it gave rise to extensive investigation of, and writing about, sectional and local history.

It was for these two concepts that Turner was best known to the general public and within the historical profession; and it was through the expression of these major concepts that Turner exercised a profound influence upon the study, writing, and teaching of United States history. Publication of the essays about the frontier and about sections kindled a broad interest in local and regional history and gave rise to a flood of publications in these areas. Moreover, Turner's interpretations of American history infused the discipline with life and peopled it with exciting characters: the story of American development became a favorite subject of popular writers. Fortunately, also, the Turner interpretation led to the reorganization and rewriting of United States history textbooks at all academic levels, truly a boon for hundreds of thousands of students. Virtually no student in the twentieth century has escaped the direct or indirect influence of Turner's work, and the "Turner thesis," and all that it implies, has become "a point of departure or reference in the same way that Max Weber's 'Protestant Ethic' or Charles Beard's 'economic interpretation' have come to be used."[7]

Perhaps, also, Turner made the study of United States history respectable; certainly, he made it popular. At a time when eminent historians at American universities were urging their students to concentrate on European history, Turner directed scholars to

America's past; he did much to develop both a knowledge and a love of country in several generations of Americans.

II *Turner the Teacher*

"No man of his generation," Louise Phelps Kellogg has observed of Turner, "did more to promote historical studies or to direct the course historical research should follow." But, Miss Kellogg hastens to add, those who had the "honor and the privilege" of studying with this man, whose suggestions changed the trend of historiography in America in one generation, "will best remember him as a teacher. . . ."[8] Carl Becker has stated, in a charming essay, that Turner's ". . . pupils understand . . . better than any others" the influence he had upon scholars.[9]

So do two of Turner's students testify to his accomplishments as a teacher. Yet, despite his pleasing platform appearance and his training in public speaking, Turner appears not to have been an outstanding classroom lecturer; and some of the students in his lecture courses on the westward movement must have found the class less than stimulating. This difficulty resulted from Turner's love of statistics—"data which belong in an appendix or perhaps in a syllabus" rather than in a lecture—and from Turner's inability to find time to prepare formal lectures.[10]

The truth of the matter seems to be that Turner found the seminar, rather than the lecture room, the nearly ideal setting for his work. In this congenial atmosphere Turner was at his best—gracious, charming, stimulating. In these seminars, Louise Kellogg has written, "we all worked together," but Turner was always "in the van of our discussions . . . guiding, suggesting, carrying over each contribution to the gathered whole, usually in a purely conversational way summing up the total of the day's result with great gusto and easy charm.[11] Turner was invariably "helpful, encouraging, and friendly." He was never sarcastic in his criticisms of students, and his "enthusiasm had a magical quality which gave significance to the history of every township, county, territory, or state" which might be the subject of a student's research paper.[12]

In the seminar, then, Turner was a master teacher. Certainly he had sufficient attributes; for, to the God-given characteristics of an engaging personality and a melodious speaking voice, he added a strong and sincere interest in each student; and he took a keen delight in watching the growth and development of his "seminarians." He brought to the seminar sessions a rarely found breadth and depth of knowledge, and he combined it with a contagious excitement which made the pursuit of historical knowledge somewhat akin to the quest for the Holy Grail.

At least two additional factors help to account for Turner's success as a teacher. First of all, he was blessed with a rich store of source material which literally surrounded his "seminarians," who usually gathered around a table located in the midst of the superb collections which Lyman C. Draper had accumulated for the State Historical Society of Wisconsin. Second, he seems to have attracted an unusually large number of serious students who were aware of the unique opportunity offered them and who took full advantage of it. A host of Turner-trained students emerged from his Wisconsin and Harvard seminars; and many of them, a surprising number, became distinguished laborers in the historical field. This large group of capable and productive scholars must surely represent Turner's greatest contribution to the academic world. Moreover, Turner "kept in touch" with many of these students, now scholars; and he always had time to offer friendly encouragement, wise counsel, and warm congratulations to his former "seminarians."

Frederick Jackson Turner was a major figure in America's academic community. As writer, teacher, and friend, he had few equals. Rarely has a historian exerted as much influence upon the course of American historiography or exercised so much influence upon the teaching of United States history. His particular genius was recognized and rewarded; accolades were heaped upon his head. Yet he was ever modest, somewhat surprised, and mildly amused about the reputation he had achieved. Throughout his life Turner was, in Carl Becker's words, ". . . a kind of intellectual Gentleman Adventurer, fascinated by 'this new world called America,' fascinated above all by the American people and by their habits of thought and action, avid for 'data' about them, wishing for his own peace of mind to understand them, to know what their 'significance' may be."[13]

Turner's contribution to the history profession was well summarized by Charles A. Beard in 1928 in a letter to Merle Curti. Beard, who had not always had complimentary remarks for Turner's efforts, wrote: "In my opinion (and you may quote this if you like), Mr. Turner deserves everlasting credit for his services as the leader in restoring the consideration of economic facts to historical writing in

America. . . . It was Mr. Turner who led in putting history on a scientific plane. Besides this, he is a scholar of fine talents and unwearying industry. His stamp is deep and indelible on historical writing in America."[14]

Ulrich B. Phillips expressed the thoughts of American historians when he wrote in his memorial to Turner that "His writings opened new vistas of knowledge; his editings gave documentation in fields of prior ignorance; his teaching inspired young scholars in remarkable number and degree; his cordial zest in comment and contribution improved the functioning of many colleagues in the craft. His life has made a lasting impress upon historical scholarship."[15]

In summary, Frederick Jackson Turner holds a secure place in American historiography. The seminal ideas which he presented brought new insights and lasting change to the study of the nation's past. He pioneered methods and techniques of investigation which opened broad new avenues to scholars in the social sciences. He demonstrated the importance of thorough study and careful research, and he did much to break down the artificial boundaries which for too long had separated the various social sciences. Through his seminars, dozens of young men and women were inspired and stimulated to set high standards for themselves, and a very high percentage of them have made lasting contributions to the profession. As a master teacher, Turner united sound research, good teaching, and the personal qualities of the true gentleman. Truly, Turner "made a lasting impress" upon the historical world.

Notes and References

Chapter One

1. Turner to Constance Lindsay Skinner, March 15, 1922, in *The Historical World of Frederick Jackson Turner with Selections from His Correspondence*, ed. Wilbur R. Jacobs (New Haven, Conn., 1968), p. 61. Hereinafter cited as *Historical World*.

2. *Ibid.*

3. Carl L. Becker, *Everyman His Own Historian, Essays on History and Politics* (New York, 1935), p. 218. Hereinafter cited as *Everyman His Own Historian*.

4. Robert G. Albion, "The Communications Revolution," *American Historical Review* XXXVII (July, 1932), 718-20.

5. Lee Benson, *Turner & Beard American Historical Writing Reconsidered* (New York, 1960), p. 43. Hereinafter cited as *Turner & Beard*.

6. See Benson, *Turner & Beard*, pp. 47-52.

7. Becker, *Everyman His Own Historian*, p. 191.

8. Merle E. Curti, "Frederick Jackson Turner," in *Wisconsin Witness to Frederick Jackson Turner: A Collection of Essays on the Historian and the Thesis*, compiled by O. Lawrence Burnette, Jr. (Madison, 1961), p. 178. Hereinafter cited as *Wisconsin Witness*.

9. *Ibid.*

10. "The Poet of the Future," *University Press* XIV (May 26, 1883), 4; "Architecture Through Oppression," *University Press* XV (June 21, 1884), 12; discussed in Curti, *Wisconsin Witness*, p. 179.

11. Turner's autobiographical letter, Jacobs, *Historical World*, pp. 59–60.

12. *State Register*, Portage, Wisconsin, June 23, 1883.

13. Turner's autobiographical letter, Jacobs, *Historical World*, p. 60.

14. Curti, "Frederick Jackson Turner," *Wisconsin Witness*, pp. 180-81.

15. Fulmer Mood, "Turner's Formative Period," in *Early Writings of Frederick Jackson Turner*, compiled by Everett E. Edwards (Madison, 1938), p. 9. Hereinafter cited as *Early Writings*.

16. Professor Marcus L. Hansen, quoted, *ibid.* Allen's untimely death shortly before he reached the age of sixty left many projects uncompleted; his published credits are not an adequate indication of his scholarly activity.

17. *Catalogue of the University of Wisconsin, 1886–87* (Madison, 1886), p. 83, quoted in Mood, "Turner's Formative Period," in *Early Writings,* p. 11.

18. Mood, "Turner's Formative Period," in *Early Writings,* p. 13. Curti, "Frederick Jackson Turner," in *Wisconsin Witness,* p. 181, states that the title of the thesis was "The Character and Influence of the Fur Trade in Wisconsin," the title under which the work was published by the State Historical Society of Wisconsin in 1889.

19. "History of the 'Grignon Tract' on the Portage of the Fox and Wisconsin Rivers," *State Register,* June 23, 1883.

20. Mood, "Turner's Formative Period," p. 19; Mood, "The Development of Frederick Jackson Turner as a Historical Thinker," *Publications of the Colonial Society of Massachusetts, Transactions* XXXIV (December, 1943), 319.

21. Mood, "Turner's Formative Period," p. 20.

22. *Ibid.;* Curti, "Frederick Jackson Turner," in *Wisconsin Witness,* p. 182.

23. Mood, "Turner's Formative Period," p. 21.

24. Mood, "The Development of Frederick Jackson Turner as a Historical Thinker," *Transactions,* pp. 320–21; Mood, "Turner's Formative Period," p. 20.

25. Letters from Turner to Allen, in Jacobs, *Historical World,* pp. 74–81.

26. *Catalogue of the University of Wisconsin, 1889-90* (Madison, 1890), p. 99; Mood, "Turner's Formative Period," pp. 24–25; Mood, "The Development of Frederick Jackson Turner as a Historical Thinker," p. 325.

27. Turner to Herbert Baxter Adams, December 10, 1889, in Jacobs, *Historical World,* p. 22.

28. *Ibid.,* p. 23.

29. Turner to Woodrow Wilson, in Jacobs, *Historical World,* pp. 24–25.

30. Woodrow Wilson to Reuben Gold Thwaites, December 26, 1889, in Jacobs, *Historical World,* p. 23.

31. Turner to Wilson, January 23, 1890, in Jacobs, *Historical World,* pp. 24–25.

32. Turner's Transcript of Courses, The Johns Hopkins University, in Mood, "Turner's Formative Period," p. 28.

33. Mood, "Turner's Formative Period," p. 29.

34. *Wisconsin Journal of Education* XXI (October, November, 1891), 23–34, 253–56.

35. "The Significance of History," *Early Writings,* pp. 66–67.

36. *Syllabus of a University Extension Course of Six Lectures on the Colonization of North America* (Madison, 1891).

37. Frederick Jackson Turner, "The Extension Work of the University of Wisconsin," *University Extension: A Monthly Journal Devoted to the Interests of Popular Education* I (April, 1892), 311–24.

38. Joseph Schafer, "Turner's Early Writing," *The Wisconsin Magazine of History* XXII (December, 1938), 216.

39. Mood, "The Development of Frederick Jackson Turner as a Historical Thinker," p. 328.

40. Emory R. Johnson, "River and Harbor Bills," American Academy of Political and Social Science, *Annals* II (May, 1892), 782–812.

41. Mood, "The Development of Frederick Jackson Turner as a Historical Thinker," pp. 329–32; Charles A. Beard, *An Economic Interpretation of the Constitution of the United States* (New York, 1913), p. 5.

Chapter Two

1. Ray Allen Billington, Foreword to *The Frontier in American History*, by Frederick Jackson Turner (New York, 1962), p. ix.

2. "The Auxiliary Congresses," *The Dial* XV (August 1, 1893), 60.

3. *Ibid*.

4. This program is discussed in the preceding chapter.

5. All references to "The Significance of History," unless otherwise noted, are to the essay as originally published in *Wisconsin Journal of Education* XXI (October, 1890), 230–34, and *Ibid*. (November, 1891), 253–56.

6. Mood, "Turner's Formative Period," p. 36.

7. "Problems in American History," *Aegis* VII (November 4, 1892), 48–52.

8. Mood, "Turner's Formative Period," pp. 37–38.

9. This summary of precursors to Turner's hypothesis is based upon Ray A. Billington, *America's Frontier Heritage* (New York, 1966), pp. 4–6. See also Lee Benson, "The Historical Background of Turner's Frontier Essay," *Agricultural History* XXV (April, 1951), 59–82; and Michael McGiffert, "Selected Writings on American National Character," *American Quarterly* XV (Summer, 1963), 270–88.

10. *Extra Census Bulletin No. 12*, April 20, 1891.

11. Turner, *Early Writings*, p. 198; Achille Loria, *Analisi della proprieta capitalista* (Turin, Italy, 1889), II, 15.

12. *Early Writings*, p. 213.

13. *Ibid*., p. 229.

14. Charles Kendall Adams, ed., *Johnson's Universal Cyclopaedia*, "A New Edition," eight vols. (New York, 1894), III, 606–7.

15. "The Problem of the West," *Atlantic Monthly* LXXXVIII (September, 1896), 289–97.

16. Ray Allen Billington, Foreword to *The Frontier in American History*, p. x.

17. *Ibid*., p. xi.

18. Chicago *Tribune*, in *ibid*., pp. x, xi.

19. Boston *Herald*, August 22, 1896, in *ibid*., p. xi.

20. "Dominant Forces in American Life," *Atlantic Monthly* LXXIX (April, 1897), 433-43; Turner, "The Middle West" *International Monthly* IV (December, 1901), 794-820; and Turner, "Contributions of the West to American Democracy," *Atlantic Monthly* XCI (January, 1903), 83-96.

21. Billington, Foreword to *The Frontier in American History*, p. xi.

22. Howard R. Lamar, "Frederick Jackson Turner," in *Pastmasters: Some Essays on American Historians*, ed. Marcus Cunliffe and Robin W. Winks (New York, 1969), p. 90.

23. Wilbur R. Jacobs, ed., *Historical World*, p. 25.

24. *Ibid.*

25. Wilson-Turner correspondence in *ibid.*, pp. 25-32.

26. Woodrow Wilson, "The Proper Perspective of American History," *Forum* XIX (July, 1895), 544-59; Woodrow Wilson, "The Making of the Nation," *Atlantic Monthly* LXXX (July, 1897), 1-14.

27. Ethel F. Fiske, ed., *The Letters of John F. Fiske* (New York, 1940), p. 693.

28. Ray Allen Billington, *America's Frontier Heritage* (New York, 1966) p. 13. The effect of the thesis on textbooks is discussed in Oscar O. Winther, "The Frontier Hypothesis and the Historian," *Social Education* XXI (November, 1957), 294-95.

29. Gene M. Gressley, "The Turner Thesis—A Problem in Historiography," *Agricultural History* XXXII (October, 1958), 230.

30. *Ibid.*

31. *Ibid.*, p. 231.

32. Merle Curti and Vernon Corstensen, *The University of Wisconsin*, two vols. (Madison, 1949), I, 643.

33. Gressley, "The Turner Thesis," p. 231.

Chapter Three

1. Lamar, "Frederick Jackson Turner," p. 92.

2. "Officers and Committees of the American Historical Association," *American Historical Review* V (April, 1900), 439.

3. Turner to J. Franklin Jameson, January 10, 1900, Turner Papers, Henry E. Huntington Library, TU Box 3. Cited in Billington, Foreword to *Rise of the New West*, by F. J. Turner, p. 10.

4. Albert B. Hart to Turner, January 2, 1902. Frederick Jackson Turner Papers, University of Wisconsin Archives, Box 1, Folder H. Cited in Billington, *ibid.*

5. Turner to Hart, January 7, 1902, *ibid.*, p. 11.

6. Hart to Turner, February 13, 1902, *ibid.*

7. Turner to Jameson, February 4, 1902, *ibid.*

8. Turner to Hart, March 8, 1902, *ibid.*, p. 12.

9. Hart to Turner, July 3, 1905, *ibid.*, p. 13.

10. Mood, "Development of Frederick Jackson Turner as a Historical

Thinker," Colonial Society of Massachusetts *Transactions*, December, 1939, p. 346.

11. Turner to Caroline Mae Turner, December 7, 1905, Turner Papers, Huntington Library, TU Box 5, *ibid.*, p. 16.

12. Hart to Max Farrand, June 2, 1922, *ibid.*, p. 19. See also Wilbur R. Jacobs, ed., *Frederick Jackson Turner's Legacy Unpublished Writings in American History* (San Marino, Calif., 1965), p. 28.

13. Lamar, "Frederick Jackson Turner," p. 92.

14. *Rise of the New West*, (New York, 1906), p. 330.

15. *Ibid.*, p. 28.

16. Mood, "Development of Frederick Jackson Turner as a Historical Thinker" p. 346.

17. *Rise of the New West*, p. 29.

18. *Ibid.*, p. xvii.

19. See reviews in *American Historical Review* XII (October, 1906), 162–64; *Literary Digest* XXXIII (September 15, 1906), 358; *Outlook*, LXXXIII (June 9, 1906), 333; and *New York Times*, April 14, May 19, 1906.

20. Lamar, "Frederick Jackson Turner," pp. 92–93.

21. Billington, Foreword, to *The Frontier in American History*, p. 7.

22. *Ibid.*

23. *Ibid.*

24. Avery Craven, "Frederick Jackson Turner, Historian," *Wisconsin Magazine of History* XXV (June, 1942), 422–23.

25. Mood, "Development of Frederick Jackson Turner as a Historical Thinker," p. 346.

26. "Draft on Sectionalism," in *Frederick Jackson Turner's Legacy*, p. 48.

27. "Introduction to a Lecture on Sectionalism," *ibid.*, p. 47; "Draft on Sectionalism" *ibid.*, p. 50.

28. "Draft on Sectionalism," *ibid.*, p. 49.

29. "The Significance of the Section," *Frontier and Section* (Englewood Cliffs, N.J., 1961), p. 118.

30. *Ibid.*

31. "Draft on Sectionalism," in *Turner's Legacy*, p. 49.

32. See Jacobs' Introduction, to *Turner's Legacy*, pp. 40–41.

33. "Draft on Sectionalism," in *Turner's Legacy*, p. 51. Turner himself experienced a kind of "culture shock" when he moved from Wisconsin to Massachusetts.

34. "Significance of the Section," in *Frontier and Section*, pp. 136–37.

35. "Sections and Nation," in *Frontier and Section*, pp. 136–37.

36. *Ibid.*, p. 138.

37. "The Significance of the Section in American History," in *Frontier and Section*, p. 135.

38. Jacobs, *Historical World*, pp. 37–39; Jacobs, ed., *Turner's Legacy*, pp. 29–30.

39. Resolution of a Committee of the Regents of the University of Wisconsin, in Jacobs, ed., *Turner's Legacy*, p. 31.

40. *Ibid.*

41. Jacobs, *Historical World*, pp. 44–45.

42. Turner to Max Farrand, October 19, 1909, quoted in Jacobs, *Historical World*, p. 45.

43. Ray Allen Billington, "Frederick Jackson Turner Comes to Harvard," *Massachusetts Historical Society Proceedings* LXXIV (1962), 52–54; see also Wilbur R. Jacobs, "Wilson's First Battle at Princeton: The Chair for Turner," *Harvard Library Bulletin* VIII (1954), 74–87.

44. Billington, "Turner Comes to Harvard," pp. 54–55.

45. *Ibid.*, p. 55.

46. *Ibid.*, pp. 55–56.

47. *Ibid.*, p. 57.

48. *Ibid.*

49. The correspondence pertinent to Jordan's offers, and to Van Hise's action at Wisconsin, is in the Turner Papers, Henry E. Huntington Library, and is the basis for Billington's discussion in *Ibid.*, pp. 61–64, to which reference is made.

50. *Ibid.*, p. 63.

51. *Ibid.*, p. 68.

52. Charles Homer Haskins to Turner, quoted in *Ibid.*, p. 71.

53. *Ibid.*, pp. 71–72.

54. Turner to Caroline Mae Turner, October 6, 1909, quoted in *Ibid.*, p. 72.

55. *Ibid.*, p. 73.

56. *Ibid.*

57. Turner to Carl Becker, December 5, 1909, quoted in *Ibid.*, p. 74.

58. *Ibid.*, pp. 74–75.

59. "Social Forces in American History," *American Historical Review* XVI (January, 1911), 232.

60. *Ibid.*, pp. 232–33.

61. *Ibid.*, p. 230.

62. *Ibid.*, p. 233.

63. Billington, Foreword to *The Frontier in American History*, p. xii.

64. Anon., "The Meeting of the American Historical Association at Indianapolis," *American Historical Review* XVI (April, 1911), 453–54.

65. Turner to Carl Becker, January 21, 1911, quoted in Jacobs, *Historical World*, pp. 134–35.

66. Turner to Becker, November 17, 1899, Becker Papers, State Historical Society of Wisconsin, quoted in Lamar, "Frederick Jackson Turner," p. 93.

67. *Ibid.*

68. Edward Everett Dale, "Memoirs of Frederick Jackson Turner," *Mississippi Valley Historical Review* XXX (December, 1943), 347.

69. *Ibid.*, pp. 339-47.

70. See Jacobs, *Historical World.*

71. Jacob E. Cooke, *Frederic Bancroft, Historian* (Norman, Okla., 1957), pp. 98-102.

72. Jacobs, *Turner's Legacy*, pp. 33-35.

73. Lamar, "Frederick Jackson Turner," pp. 95-96.

74. *Ibid.*

75. See, for example, Turner to Joseph Jastrow, October 5, 1910, in Jacobs, *Historical World*, pp. 47-49.

76. See *Ibid.*, pp. 221-30 for two examples of this.

77. Jacobs, *Historical World*, pp. 143-49, 101-6.

78. Turner to Eugene H. Roseboom, November 22, 1923, in Jacobs, *Historical World*, pp. 228-30.

79. *Ibid.*, pp. 62-66.

80. Lamar, "Frederick Jackson Turner," p. 99; Roy M. Robbins, "Review of *The United States 1830-1850: The Nation and Its Sections,*" *Mississippi Valley Historical Review* XXII (September, 1935). 295-97.

Chapter Four

1. Edmond S. Meany, "The Towns of the Pacific Northwest Were Not Founded on the Fur Trade," American Historical Association, *Annual Report*, 1909 (Washington, 1911), pp. 165-72.

2. *Rise of the New West, 1819-1829*, vol. XIV of *The American Nation: A History*, 28 vols. (New York, 1904-1918), pp. 113-14.

3. Meany, "The Towns of the Pacific Northwest," p. 166.

4. *Ibid.*, p. 172.

5. Gene M. Gressley, "The Turner Thesis—A Problem in Historiography," *Agricultural History* XXII (October, 1958), 231.

6. Charles A. Beard, "The Frontier in American History," *The New Republic* XXV (February, 16, 1921), 349-50.

7. *Ibid.*, p. 349.

8. *Ibid.*

9. *Ibid.*, p. 350.

10. *The Frontier in American History* (New York, 1920), p. 12.

11. Clarence W. Alvard, "Review of Frederick Jackson Turner's *The Frontier in American History,*" *Mississippi Valley Historical Review* VII (March, 1921), 403-7.

12. John C. Almack, "The Shibboleth of the Frontier," *Historical Outlook* XVI (May, 1925), 202.

13. John Carl Parish, "The Persistence of the Westward Movement," *Yale Review* XV (April, 1926), 461-77.

14. Ray Allen Billington, *The Frontier Thesis, Valid Interpretation of American History?* (New York, 1966), p. 3.

15. Quoted in Billington, *America's Frontier Heritage*, p. 14.

16. See Norman Foerster, "American Literature," *Saturday Review of Literature* II (April 3, 1926), 677–79.

17. Madison, Wisconsin *Capital Times*, January 15, 1931, quoted in Billington, *America's Frontier Heritage*, p. 15.

18. Billington, *America's Frontier Heritage*, p. 15; Curtis Nettels, "Frederick Jackson Turner and the New Deal," *Wisconsin Magazine of History* XVII (March, 1934), 257–65; and William A. Williams, "The Frontier Thesis and American Foreign Policy," *Pacific Historical Review* XXIV (November, 1955), 379–95.

19. Billington, *The Frontier Thesis*, p. 3.

20. Billington, *America's Frontier Heritage*, pp. 15–16.
See also Warren I. Susman, "The Useless Past: American Intellectuals and the Frontier Thesis: 1910–1930," *Bucknell Review* XI (March, 1963), 1–20.

21. Benjamin F. Wright, "American Democracy and the Frontier," *Yale Review* XX (December, 1930), 349–65.

22. Benjamin F. Wright, "Political Institutions and the Frontier," in *Sources of Culture in the Middle West*, ed. Dixon R. Fox (New York, 1934), pp. 15–38; Benjamin F. Wright, "Review of Frederick J. Turner's *Significance of Sections in American History*," *New England Quarterly* VI (September, 1933), 630–34.

23. Louis M. Hacker, "Sections or Classes," *The Nation* CXXXVII (July 26, 1933), 108–10. Time changes interpretation, as Professor George W. Pierson once noted. Hacker's views subsequently were softened by the late 1940s. See Louis M. Hacker, *The Shaping of the American Tradition*, 2 vols. (New York, 1947), I, xv–xxiv.

24. Charles A. Beard, "The Frontiers in American History," *New Republic* XCVII (February 1, 1939), 359–62.

25. Gressley, "The Turner Thesis," p. 234.

26. George W. Pierson, "Recent Studies of Turner and the Frontier Doctrine," *Mississippi Valley Historical Review* XXXIV (December, 1947), 453–58.

27. Carter Goodrich and Sol Davison, "The Wage-Earner in the Westward Movement," *Political Science Quarterly* L (June, 1935), 161–85, and *ibid.*, LI (March, 1936), 61–116.

28. *Ibid.*; Gressley, "The Turner Thesis," p. 234.

29. Fred A. Shannon, "The Homestead Act and the Labor Surplus," *American Historical Review* XLI (July, 1936), 637–51.

30. Murray Kane, "Some Considerations on the Safety-Valve Doctrine," *Mississippi Valley Historical Review* XXIII (September, 1936), 169–88.

31. The defense of the Turner thesis is considered in more detail later in this chapter.

32. Carter Goodrich and Sol Davison, "The Frontier as a Safety-Valve: A Rejoinder," *Political Science Quarterly* LIII (June, 1938), 268–71.

33. Fred A. Shannon, "A Post Mortem on the Labor-Safety-Valve Theory," *Agricultural History* XIX (January, 1945), 31–38.

34. Norman J. Simler, "The Safety Valve Doctrine Re-Evaluated," *Agricultural History* XXXII (October, 1958), 252.

35. *Ibid.*

36. *Ibid.*, p. 253.

37. *Ibid.*, p. 255.

38. *Ibid.*, p. 256.

39. Fred A. Shannon, "To the Editor," *Agricultural History* XXXII (October, 1958), 257.

40. Thomas P. Abernethy, *Frontier to Plantation* (Chapel Hill, N.C., 1932), p. 362.

41. Arthur M. Schlesinger, Sr., "The City in American History," *Mississippi Valley Historical Review* XXVII (June, 1940), 43-67. See also the same author's *The Rise of the City, 1878-1898* (New York, 1933).

42. Gressley, "The Turner Thesis," p. 236.

43. Murray Kane, "Some Considerations on the Frontier Concept of Frederick Jackson Turner," *Mississippi Valley Historical Review* XXVII (December, 1940), 379-400.

44. George W. Pierson, "The Frontier and the Frontiersmen of Turner's Essays," *Pennsylvania Magazine of History and Biography* LXIV (October, 1940), 478. See also George W. Pierson, "The Frontier and American Institutions—A Criticism of the Turner Theory," *New England Quarterly* XV (June, 1942), 224-55; George W. Pierson, "American Historians and the Frontier Thesis in 1941," *Wisconsin Magazine of History* XXVI (September, 1942), 36-60, and *ibid.* (December, 1942). 170-85; and George W. Pierson, "Recent Studies of Turner and the Frontier Doctrine," *Mississippi Valley Historical Review* XXXIV (December, 1947), 452-58.

45. Carlton J. H. Hayes, "American Frontier—Frontier of What?" *American Historical Review* LI (January, 1946), 199-210.

46. James C. Malin, *Essays on Historiography* (Lawrence, Kansas, 1946), pp. 1-44.

47. Henry Nash Smith, *Virgin Land: The American West as Symbol and Myth* (Cambridge, 1950), pp. 259-60.

48. Richard Hofstadter, "Turner and the Frontier Myth," *The American Scholar* XVIII (October, 1949), 433-43.

49. Richard Hofstadter, *The Age of Reform From Bryan to F. D. R.* (New York, 1955), p. 37.

50. Hofstadter, "Turner and the Frontier Myth," p. 440.

51. Frederic L. Paxson, *The Last American Frontier* (New York, 1910), p. 3.

52. Frederic L. Paxson, *The History of the American Frontier, 1763-1893* (Boston, 1924), p. 573.

53. Carl Becker, "Frederick Jackson Turner," in *American Masters of Social Science*, ed. Howard W. Odum (New York, 1927), pp. 273-318.

54. *Ibid.*, p. 317.

55. Merle Curti, "The Section and the Frontier in American History:

The Methodological Concepts of Frederick Jackson Turner," in *Methods in Social Science*, ed. Stuart A. Rice (Chicago, 1931), pp. 353-67.

56. Joseph Schafer, "Turner's Frontier Philosophy," *Wisconsin Magazine of History* XVI (June, 1933), 451-69; Joseph Schafer, "Turner's America," *Wisconsin Magazine of History* XVII (June 1934), 447-65.

57. Howard R. Lamar, "Frederick Jackson Turner," p. 101.

58. Louis Hacker, "Sections or Classes," *The Nation* CXXXVII (July, 1933), 108-10.

59. Avery O. Craven, "Frederick Jackson Turner," in *Marcus W. Jernegan Essays in American Historiography*, ed. William T. Hutchinson (Chicago, 1937), pp. 252-70.

60. *Ibid.*, pp. 258-59.

61. Avery O. Craven, "Turner Theories and the South," *Journal of Southern History* V (August, 1939), 295.

62. Avery O. Craven, "Frederick Jackson Turner, Historian," *Wisconsin Magazine of History* XXV (June, 1942), 408-24.

63. Avery O. Craven, "Frederick Jackson Turner and the Frontier Approach," *University of Kansas City Review* XVIII (Autumn, 1951), 16.

64. Ray A. Billington and James B. Hedges, *Westward Expansion A History of the American Frontier* (New York, 1949).

65. *Ibid.*, p. vii.

66. Homer C. Hockett did not agree with the general evaluation of the book. See his review of *Westward Expansion* in *Mississippi Valley Historical Review* XXXVI (December, 1949), 550-52.

67. Walter Prescott Webb, *The Great Frontier* (Boston, 1952).

68. *Ibid.*, p. 415. Not surprisingly, *The Great Frontier* attracted much discussion, as had his earlier volume, *The Great Plains* (New York, 1931). The following are enlightening in this respect: J. H. Hexter, Review of Walter P. Webb *The Great Frontier*, *American Historical Review* LVIII (July, 1953), 963; Ray A. Billington, Review of Walter P. Webb *The Great Frontier*, *Mississippi Valley Historical Review* XL (June, 1953), 107-8; Henry S. Commager, "Historical Writings," *The London Times Literary Supplement*, January 6, 1956; Geoffrey Barraclough, *History In A Changing World* (Oxford, 1955); and John D. Hicks, Review of Walter P. Webb *The Great Frontier*, *Saturday Review of Literature* XXXV (December 27, 1952), 10-11. In identifying with the Progressive aim of using government as a new force to sustain democracy, a function formerly performed by the frontier, Turner may have anticipated Webb.

69. John D. Barnhart, *Valley of Democracy: The Frontier Versus the Plantation in the Ohio Valley, 1775-1818* (Bloomington, Indiana, 1953).

70. Stanley Elkins and Eric McKitrick, "A Meaning for Turner's Frontier," *Political Science Quarterly* LXIX (September, December, 1954), 321-53, 565-602.

71. *Ibid.*, p. 602.

72. Quoted in Gressley, "The Turner Thesis," p. 247.

73. Merle Curti, *The Making of An American Community: A Case Study of Democracy in a Frontier County* (Stanford, California, 1959), p. 448. Also see Merle Curti, "The Democratic Theme in American Historical Literature," *Mississippi Valley Historical Review* XXXIX (June, 1952), 3–28; and Merle Curti, *Probing Our Past* (New York, 1955).

74. Peter J. Coleman, "The New Zealand Frontier and the Turner Thesis," *Pacific Historical Review* XXVII (August, 1958), 221–37.

75. Marvin W. Mikesell, "Comparative Studies in Frontier History," Association of American Geographers, *Annals* L (March, 1960), 62–74.

76. Staughton Lynd, "On Turner, Beard and Slavery," *Journal of Negro History* XLVIII (October, 1963), 235–50.

77. *Ibid.*, p. 235.

78. The thesis continues to be accepted, in large degree, by most college textbooks on United States history. See Gressley, "The Turner Thesis," p. 249. The quotation is in *ibid.*, n. 120.

Chapter Five

1. Quoted in Ray Allen Billington, "Frederick Jackson Turner—Universal Historian," in Frederick Jackson Turner, *Frontier and Section Selected Essays of Frederick Jackson Turner* (Englewood Cliffs, N.J., 1961), p. 2.

2. *Ibid.*

3. Wilbur R. Jacobs, John W. Caughey, and Joe B. Frantz, *Turner, Bolton, and Webb, Three Historians of the American Frontier* (Seattle, 1965), p. 26.

4. Billington, "Frederick Jackson Turner—Universal Historian," p. 1.

5. Howard R. Lamar, "Frederick Jackson Turner," p. 74.

6. S. E. Morison, "Frederick Jackson Turner (1861–1932)," American Academy of Arts and Sciences, *Proceedings* LXVIII (1933), 685–86.

7. Lamar, "Frederick Jackson Turner," p. 101.

8. Louis Phelps Kellogg, "The Passing of a Great Teacher—Frederick Jackson Turner," *The Historical Outlook* XXIII (October, 1932), 270–72.

9. Carl Becker, "Frederick Jackson Turner," in *American Masters of Social Science*, ed. Howard W. Odum (Port Washington, N.Y., 1927), p. 317.

10. See Ulrich Bonnell Phillips, "The Traits and Contributions of Frederick Jackson Turner," *Agricultural History* XIX (January, 1945), 21–23.

11. Kellogg, *ibid.*, p. 270.

12. Wilbur R. Jacobs, "Frederick Jackson Turner—Master Teacher," *Pacific Historical Review* XXIII (February, 1954), 49–58.

13. Becker, "Frederick Jackson Turner," p. 316.

14. Charles A. Beard to Merle Curti, August 9, 1928; quoted in Jacobs, *Turner's Legacy*, pp. 36–37.

15. Ulrich B. Phillips, "Memorial to Frederick Jackson Turner," American Historical Association, *Annual Report*, 1932, p. 55.

Selective Bibliography

PRIMARY SOURCES

Note: The most nearly complete listing of Turner's writings, compiled by Everett E. Edwards, is in *Early Writings of Frederick Jackson Turner*, compiled by Everett E. Edwards, Madison, Wisconsin: University of Wisconsin Press, 1938.

1. Books

Frontier and Section: Selected Essays of Frederick Jackson Turner. Edited by Ray A. Billington. Englewood Cliffs, N.J.: Prentice Hall, 1961.

Rise of the New West, 1819–1829. New York: Harper, 1906.

The Character and Influence of the Indian Trade in Wisconsin: A Study of the Trading Post as an Institution. Johns Hopkins University Studies in Historical and Political Science, 9th series, nos. 11–12. Baltimore: Johns Hopkins Press, 1891.

The Frontier in American History. New York: Henry Holt, 1920.

The Significance of Sections in American History. Introduction by Max Farrand. New York: Henry Holt, 1932.

The United States, 1830–1850: The Nation and Its Sections. Introduction by Avery Craven. New York: Henry Holt, 1935.

2. Articles

"Architecture Through Oppression." *University Press* (Madison, Wisconsin), June 21, 1884.

"Carondelet on the Defence of Louisiana, 1794." *American Historical Review* II (April, 1897), 474–505.

"Clark-Genet Correspondence: Selections from the Draper Collection in the Possession of the State Historical Society of Wisconsin, to Elucidate the Proposed French Expedition under George Rogers Clark against Louisiana in the Years 1793–94." American Historical Association, *Annual Report,* 1896, I, 930–1107. Washington: Government Printing Office, 1897.

"Contributions of the West to American Democracy." *Atlantic Monthly* LXXXXI (January, 1903), 83–96.

"Correspondence of the French Ministers to the United States, 1791–1797." (ed.), American Historical Association, *Annual Report,* 1903, vol. II. Washington: Government Printing Office, 1904.

"Documents on the Blount Conspiracy, 1795-1797." *American Historical Review* X (April, 1905), 574-606.

"Documents on the Relations of France to Louisiana, 1792-1795." *American Historical Review* III (April, 1898), 490-516.

"Dominant Forces in Western Life." *Atlantic Monthly* LXXIX (April, 1897), 433-43.

"English Policy Toward America in 1790-1791." *American Historical Review* VII (July, October, 1902), 706-35, 78-86.

"Frontier." *Johnson's Universal Cyclopaedia* (New York: A. J. Johnson Co., 1894), III, 606-7.

"Geographic Sectionalism in American History." Association of American Geographers, *Annals* XVI (June, 1926), 85-93.

"Geographical Interpretations of American History." *Journal of Geography* IV (January, 1905), 34-37.

"George Rogers Clark and the Kaskaskia Campaign, 1777-1778." *American Historical Review* VIII (April, 1903), 491-506.

"Greater New England in the Middle of the Nineteenth Century," American Antiquarian Society, *Proceedings,* XXIX (October 15, 1919), 222-41.

"History of the 'Grignon Tract' on the Portage of the Fox and Wisconsin Rivers." *State Register* (Portage, Wisconsin), June 23, 1883.

"Is Sectionalism in America Dying Away?" *American Journal of Sociology* XIII (March, 1908), 661-75.

"Jefferson to George Rogers Clark, 1783." *American Historical Review* III (July, 1898), 672-73.

"Middle Western Pioneer Democracy." *Minnesota History Bulletin* III (August, 1920), 393-414.

"On the Relations of Geography to History." American Historical Association, *Annual Report,* 1908, I, 61. Washington: Government Printing Office, 1909.

"On Research in Southern History." American Historical Association, *Annual Report,* 1908, I, 131-43. Washington: Government Printing Office, 1909.

"Pioneer Ideals and the State University." *Indiana University Bulletin* VIII (June 15, 1910), 6-29.

"Problems in American History." *Aegis* VII (November 4, 1892), 48-52.

"Problems in American History." In *International Congress of Arts and Science, Universal Exposition, St. Louis,* edited by Howard J. Rogers, II, 183-94. Boston: Houghton Mifflin, 1906.

"Report of the Conference on the Relation of Geography and History." American Historical Association, *Annual Report,* 1907. Washington: Government Printing Office, 1908.

"Sectionalism in the United States." In *Cyclopedia of American Government,* edited by Andrew C. McLaughlin and Albert B. Hart, III, 280-85. New York: D. Appleton, 1914.

"Sections and Nation." *Yale Review* XII (October, 1922), 1-21.
"Since the Foundation of Clark University, 1889-1924." *Historical Outlook* XV (November, 1924), 335-42.
"Social Forces in American History." *American Historical Review* XVI (January, 1911), 217-33.
"Studies of American Immigration." *Chicago Record-Herald*, August 28, September 4, 11, 18, 25, October 16, 1901.
"The Character and Influence of the Fur Trade in Wisconsin." Wisconsin Historical Society, *Proceedings* I (1889), 52-98.
"The Children of the Pioneers." *Yale Review* XV (July, 1926), 645-70.
"The Colonization of the West, 1820-1830." *American Historical Review* XI (January, 1906), 303-27.
"The Democratic Education of the Middle West." *World's Work* VI (August, 1903), 3754-59.
"The Development of American Society." University of Illinois *Alumni Quarterly* II (July, 1908), 120-36.
"The Diplomatic Contest for the Mississippi Valley." *Atlantic Monthly* LXXXXIII (May, June, 1904), 676-91, 807-17.
"The Extension Work of the University of Wisconsin." *Handbook of University Extension*, no. 1, being vol. I of *University Extension* (Philadelphia, 1892), pp. 311-24.
"The First Official Frontier of the Massachusetts Bay." *Publications of the Colonial Society of Massachusetts, Transactions*, XVII (1913-14), 250-71.
"The Harvard Commission on Western History." *Harvard Graduates' Magazine* XX (June, 1912), 606-11.
"The Historical Library in the University." *The Dedication of the Library Building May the Seventeenth*, pp. 41-58. Providence, Rhode Island: Brown University, 1905.
"The Intellectual Influence of the West Upon the Nation." *Minnesota Daily*, June 7, 1900.
"The Mangourit Correspondence in Respect to Genet's Projected Attack Upon the Floridas, 1793-94." American Historical Association, *Annual Report*, 1897, pp. 569-679. Washington: Government Printing Office, 1898.
"The Middle West." *International Monthly* IV (December, 1901), 794-820.
"The Old West." Wisconsin State Historical Society, *Proceedings* LVI (January, 1908), 184-233.
"The Origin of Genet's Projected Attack on Louisiana and the Floridas." *American Historical Review* III (July, 1898), 650-71.
"The Place of the Ohio Valley in American History. *Ohio Archaeological and Historical Quarterly* XX (January, 1911), 32-47.
"The Poet of the Future." *University Press* (Madison, Wisconsin), May 26, 1883.
"The Policy of France Toward the Mississippi Valley in the Period of

Washington and Adams." *American Historical Review* X (January, 1905), 249-79.

"The Problem of the West." *Atlantic Monthly* LXXVIII (September, 1896), 289-97.

"The Rise and Fall of New France." *Chautauquan* XXIV (October, December, 1896), 31-34, 295-300.

"The Significance of History." *Wisconsin Journal of Education* XXI (October, November, 1891), 230-34, 253-56.

"The Significance of the Frontier in American History." American Historical Association, *Annual Report*, 1892, pp. 199-227. Washington: Government Printing Office, 1893.

"The Significance of the Louisiana Purchase." *American Monthly Review of Reviews* XXVII (May, 1903), 578-84.

"The Significance of the Mississippi Valley in American History." Mississippi Valley Historical Association, *Proceedings*, III (1911), 159-84.

"The Significance of the Section in American History." *Wisconsin Magazine of History* VIII (March, 1925), 255-80.

"The South, 1820-1830." *American Historical Review* XI (April, 1906), 559-73.

"The West and American Ideals." *Washington Historical Quarterly* V (October, 1914), 243-57.

"The West As a Field for Historical Study." American Historical Association, *Annual Report*, 1896, I, 281-87. Washington: Government Printing Office, 1897.

"The West—1876 and 1926: Its Progress in a Half-Century." *World's Work* LII (July, 1926), 319-27.

"Turner's Autobiographic Letter." *Wisconsin Magazine of History* XIX (September, 1935), 91-103.

"West As a Factor in American Politics." In *Cyclopedia of American Government*, edited by Andrew C. McLaughlin and Albert B. Hart, III, 668-75. New York: D. Appleton, 1914.

"Western State-Making in the Revolutionary Era." *American Historical Review* I (October, 1895; January, 1896), 70-87, 251-69.

"Wisconsin." *Encyclopedia Britannica*, 9th ed., XXIV, 616-19. Chicago: The Werner Co., 1893.

3.   Reviews of Books

Brown, Alexander. *English Politics in Early Virginia History* (Boston, 1901), in *American Historical Review* VII (October, 1901), 159-63.

Burgess, J. W. *The Middle Period, 1817—1858* (New York, 1897), in *Educational Review* XIV (November, 1897), 390-95.

Channing, Edward. *A Students' History of the United States* (New York, 1898), in *Educational Review* XVIII (October, 1899), 301-4.

Chittenden, H. M. *History of Early Steamboat Navigation on the Missouri River: Life and Adventures of Joseph La Barge* (New York, 1903), in *American Historical Review* XI (January, 1906), 443-44.

Coues, Elliott, ed. *New Light on the Early History of the Greater North-west: The Manuscript Journals of Alexander Henry . . . and of David Thompson . . . 1799—1814. Exploration and Adventure Among the Indians on the Red, Saskatchewan, Missouri, and Columbia Rivers.* Edited with Copious Critical Commentary (New York, 1897), in *American Historical Review* III (October, 1897), 157-59.

"Crossing the Continent." *Dial* XVI (February 1, 1894), 80-82.

English, W. H. *Conquest of the Country Northwest of the River Ohio, 1778-1783; and Life of Gen. George Rogers Clark* (Indianapolis, Indiana, 1896), in *American Historical Review* II (January, 1897), 363-66.

"Franklin in France." *Dial* VIII (May, 1887), 7-10.

Gordy, J. P. *A History of Political Parties in the United States* (Athens, Ohio, 1895), in *Political Science Quarterly* XII (March, 1897), 163-64.

Hosmer, J. K. *A Short History of the Mississippi Valley.* (Boston, 1901), in *American Historical Review*, VII (July, 1902), 801-03.

"The Journal of a Pennsylvania Senator." *Dial* XII (July, 1891), 78-81.

Judson, H. P. *The Growth of the American Nation* (Meadville, Pa., 1895), in *American Historical Review* I (April, 1896), 549-50.

"A New History of America." *Dial* XIII (December 16, 1892), 389-91.

Parkman, Francis. *Francis Parkman's Works* (Boston, 1898), in *Dial* XXV (December 16, 1898), 451-53.

"Recent Studies in American History." *Atlantic Monthly* LXXVII (June, 1896), 837-44.

Rhodes, J. F. *History of the United States from the Compromise of 1850* (New York, 1895), in *Political Science Quarterly* II (March, 1896), 167-70.

Roosevelt, Theodore. *The Winning of the West* (New York, 1896), in *American Historical Review* II (October, 1896), 171-76.

Thwaites, Ruben G. *Early Western Travels, 1748-1846* (Cleveland, 1904), in *Dial* XXVII (November 16, 1904), 298-302.

Trevelyan, G. O. *The American Revolution* (New York, 1899), in *American Historical Review* V (October, 1899), 141-44.

Wilson, Woodrow. *A History of the American People* (New York, 1902), in *American Historical Review* VIII (July, 1903), 762-65.

"The Winning of the West." *Dial* X (August, 1889), 71-73.

Winslow, J. B. *The Story of a Great Court: Being a Sketch History of the Supreme Court of Wisconsin* (Chicago, 1912), in *American Historical Review* XVII (July, 1912), 859-60.

Winsor, Justin. *The Westward Movement* (Boston, 1897), in *American Historical Review* III (April, 1898), 556-61.

4. Miscellaneous

American Development, 1789-1829: Syllabus of a Course of Six Lectures. Madison, Wisconsin: Tracy, Gibbs, 1895.

The Colonization of North America From the Earliest Times to 1763: Syl-

labus of a Course of Six Lectures. Madison, Wisconsin: Tracy, Gibbs, 1893.

The Conquest and Organization of the Northwest Territory Teachers' Course of Lectures on American History in the Hall of the Washington High School, 7th and O Sts., N. W. Washington, D. C., 1889.

Guide to the Study and Reading of American History (with Edward Channing and Albert B. Hart), Boston: Ginn, 1912.

A Half Century of American Politics, 1789-1840: Syllabus of a Course of Six Lectures. Madison, Wisconsin: Tracy, Gibbs, 1894.

List of References on the History of the West (With Frederick Merk). Cambridge, Mass., Harvard University Press, 1922.

Outline Studies in the History of the Northwest. Chicago: National Bureau of Unity Club, 1888.

State Register. Portage, Wisconsin, 1883. Turner's earliest publication is carried here.

Suggestive Outlines for the Study of the History of the Middle West, Kentucky, and Tennessee. State Historical Society of Wisconsin, Bulletin of Information no. 15. Madison, Wisconsin, Democrat Printing Co., 1901.

Syllabus of a University Extension Course of Six Lectures on the Colonization of North America. Madison, Wisconsin, 1891.

U. S. Committee on Department Methods: Message from the President of the United States, Transmitting a Report by the Committee on Department Methods on the Documentary Historical Publications of the United States Government, together with a Draft of a Proposed Bill Providing for the Creation of a Permanent Commission on National Historical Publications. Sixtieth Congress, 2d sess. S. Doc. No. 714. Washington, D.C. : Government Printing Office, 1909.

University Extension: A Monthly Journal Devoted to the Interests of Popular Education, April, 1892, University of Wisconsin. Contains Turner's article on the uses of history written for the University's extension program.

Wisconsin Journal of Education XXI (October, November, 1891), 23-34, 253-56. Contains Turner's essay on the significance of history.

SECONDARY SOURCES
1. Books

ABERNETHY, THOMAS P. *Frontier to Plantation.* Chapel Hill, North Carolina: University of North Carolina Press, 1932. Useful study of the frontier process in the Southwest.

BARNHART, JOHN D. *Valley of Democracy: The Frontier Versus the Plantation in the Ohio Valley, 1775-1818.* Bloomington, Indiana: Indiana University Press, 1953. A "testing of the Turner interpretation by an application to a specific area and time." Findings supported Turner's interpretations. See especially the final chapter.

BARRACLOUGH, GEOFFREY. *History in a Changing World.* Oxford: Blackwell, 1955. Does not accept wholeheartedly much of Webb's *The Great Frontier;* considered it a good illustration that present is not simply a continuation of the past.

BEARD, CHARLES A. *An Economic Interpretation of the Constitution of the United States.* New York: Macmillan, 1913. Outstanding example of interpretative history; work has become a classic in United States history.

BECKER, CARL L. *Everyman His Own Historian, Essays On History and Politics.* New York: Appleton-Century-Crofts, 1935. Becker's charming and beautifully written essay on his former teacher is included in this volume. The essay explains the influence which Turner exerted upon his graduate students and describes the professor's seminar method.

BENSON, LEE. *Turner & Beard, Historical Writing Reconsidered.* New York: The Free Press, 1960. Benson discusses the historical background of the frontier essay, and presents Achille Loria's economic thought and Loria's "contribution to the frontier hypothesis."

BILLINGTON, RAY A. *America's Frontier Heritage.* New York: Holt, Rinehart and Winston, 1966. This excellent book is a reappraisal of the "entire frontier hypothesis in the light of modern research in both history and the social sciences." It meets admirably the high standards readers have come to expect from Billington.

——. *Frederick Jackson Turner Historian, Scholar, Teacher.* New York: Oxford University Press, 1973. Definitive study of Turner.

——. *The Genesis of the Frontier Thesis: A Study in Historical Creativity.* San Marino, Calif.: Huntington Library, 1971. Considers forces which helped Turner form the frontier thesis.

——, ed. *The Frontier Thesis Valid Interpretation of American History?* New York: Holt, Rinehart and Winston, 1966. Brings together in this brief work some of the major essays dealing with the Turner thesis and with the safety-valve theory. Concludes with two summary essays, one upholding and one attacking the thesis.

——, and JAMES B. HEDGES. *Westward Expansion A History of the American Frontier.* 3d ed. New York: Macmillan, 1967. The best account of the westward movement across the continent; combines sound research and pleasing style; and bibliography is in itself an outstanding contribution to historiography.

BURNETTE, O. LAWRENCE, compiler. *Wisconsin Witness to Frederick Jackson Turner: A Collection of Essays on the Historian and the Thesis.* Madison, Wisconsin: The State Historical Society of Wisconsin, 1961.

Good collection of essays, contributed by outstanding historians, dealing with Turner and his writings.

COOKE, JACOB E. *Frederic Bancroft, Historian.* Norman, Oklahoma: University of Oklahoma Press, 1957. Useful material on Bancroft.

CURTI, MERLE. *The Making of An American Community: A Case Study of Democracy in a Frontier County.* Stanford, California: Stanford University Press, 1959. "In-depth" study of a frontier county using modern research methods to study democracy as it developed in a frontier community.

———. *Probing Our Past.* New York: Harper, 1955. Additional ideas concerning the frontier and democracy.

———, and VERNON CORSTENSEN. *The University of Wisconsin.* Two volumes, Madison, Wisconsin: University of Wisconsin Press, 1949. Excellent source on the university and Turner's association with it.

EDWARDS, EVERETT E., compiler. *Early Writings of Frederick Jackson Turner.* Madison, Wisconsin: University of Wisconsin Press, 1938. Contains Fulmer Mood's "Turner's Formative Period" and Edwards's compilation of Turner's writing.

FISKE, ETHEL F., ed. *The Letters of John F. Fiske.* New York: Macmillan, 1940. Gives some indication of the popularity of Turner's ideas.

HACKER, LOUIS M. *The Shaping of the American Tradition.* Two volumes, New York: Columbia University Press, 1947. Dr. Hacker was considerably less opposed to the frontier thesis in 1947 than he had been in 1933 when he wrote "Sections or Classes," *The Nation* CXXXVII (July, 1933), 108–10. By the latter date he was willing to accept the theory as a partial explanation of the development of American life.

HOFSTADTER, RICHARD. *The Age of Reform From Bryan to F. D. R.* New York: Vintage Books, 1955. This extremely provocative study considers the "agrarian myth" and concludes that it has been destroyed by the triumph of commercial agriculture.

JACOBS, WILBUR R., ed. *Frederick Jackson Turner's Legacy, Unpublished Writings in American History.* San Marino, California: The Huntington Library, 1965. This and the following volume contain essays, lectures, and letters from the Turner Papers at the Henry E. Huntington Library and Art Gallery. This collection was opened to scholars in 1960. Both volumes provide judiciously selected materials dealing with Turner's personal and professional life.

———. *The Historical World of Frederick Jackson Turner.* With Selections From His Correspondence. New Haven, Connecticut: Yale University Press, 1968. Fine collection of Turner's letters.

LORIA, ACHILLE. *Analisi della proprieta capitalista.* Turin, Italy, 1889. The theories of this Italian economist were known to Turner, and they probably influenced his work.

MALIN, JAMES C. *Essays on Historiography.* Lawrence, Kansas: J. C. Malin, 1946. These essays present disagreement with Turner based upon what Malin felt was Turner's "peculiar absorption" with the closed space doctrine.

PAXSON, FREDERIC L. *The History of the American Frontier, 1763–1893.* Boston: Houghton Mifflin, 1924. Here, and in his *The Last American Frontier*, this distinguished historian of the frontier presents his views and his doubts and questions about Turner's theory.

———. *The Last American Frontier.* New York: Macmillan, 1910. Presents Paxson's views on the Turner thesis.

SCHLESINGER, ARTHUR M. SR. *The Rise of the City, 1878–1898.* New York: Macmillan, 1933. Stresses the importance of the urban viewpoint in the development of the United States. His 1940 article in the *Mississippi Valley Historical Review* opened that decade's attack on the frontier theory.

SMITH, HENRY NASH. *Virgin Land: The American West As Symbol and Myth.* Cambridge, Massachusetts: Harvard University Press, 1950. Smith found what he thought were inconsistencies in Turner's work and believed that overemphasis on the frontier theory had given rise to an "agrarian myth" which presented an unbalanced view of the country's development.

WEBB, WALTER PRESCOTT. *The Great Frontier.* Boston: Houghton Mifflin, 1952. In common with his earlier volume, *The Great Plains*, this volume was the subject of bitter controversy. The book, which Webb said would not be understood for many years, explored the frontier concept in a worldwide setting. Recent scholarship attests to the significance of Webb's ideas.

———. *The Great Plains.* New York: Ginn, 1931. This volume, stressing the uniqueness of a geographical region of the United States, suggested the importance of negative factors in the development of the region. An extremely provocative book, it occasioned a great deal of debate and marked Webb as an original thinker in the field of United States history.

2. Articles

ALBION, ROBERT G. "The Communications Revolution." *American Historical Review* XXXVII (July, 1932), 718–20. Stimulating essay.

ALMACK, JOHN C. "The Shibboleth of the Frontier." *Historical Outlook* XVI (May, 1925), 197–202. Presents arguments against the Turner thesis.

ALVARD, CLARENCE W. Review of Frederick Jackson Turner *The Frontier in American History. Mississippi Valley Historical Review* VII (March, 1921), 403–7. Takes issue with some of Turner's ideas.

AMERICAN ACADEMY OF POLITICAL AND SOCIAL SCIENCE. *Annals* II (May, 1892), 782–83. Of limited use.

BEARD, CHARLES A. "The Frontier in American History." *New Republic* XXV (February 16, 1921), 349–50. Beard presents criticisms of the Turner thesis.

————. "The Frontier in American History." *New Republic* XCVII (February 1, 1939), 359–62. Beard presents his views on the role of the frontier in American history.

BECKER, CARL. "Frederick Jackson Turner." *In American Masters of Social Science,* ed. Howard W. Odum (New York: Henry Holt, 1927). Warm, perceptive treatment of Turner by one of his students.

BILLINGTON, RAY A. Foreword to *The Frontier in American History.* New York: Holt, Rinehart and Winston, 1962. Contributes to a better understanding of Turner and his work.

————. "Frederick Jackson Turner Comes to Harvard." Massachusetts Historical Society, *Proceedings* LXXIV (1962), 51–83. Useful discussion of this major event in Turner's life.

————. "Frederick Jackson Turner—Universal Historian." In *Frontier and Section: Selected Essays of Frederick Jackson Turner.* Englewood Cliffs, New Jersey: Prentice Hall, 1961. Extremely helpful introduction to these important essays.

————. "Review of Walter P. Webb's *The Great Frontier.*" *Mississippi Valley Historical Review* XL (June, 1953), 107–8. Thoughtful review of an important book.

COLEMAN, PETER J. "The New Zealand Frontier and the Turner Thesis." *Pacific Historical Review* XXVII (August, 1958), 221–37. One of several attempts to apply the Turner thesis to other countries.

COLEMAN, WILLIAM. "Science and Symbol in the Turner Frontier Hypothesis." *American Historical Review* LXXII (October, 1966), 22–49. Study of developments in biology and geography which influenced Turner's thought.

COMMAGER, HENRY S. "Historical Writings." *The London Times Literary Supplement,* January 6, 1956. Helpful commentary.

CRAVEN, AVERY O. "Frederick Jackson Turner." In *Marcus W. Jernegan Essays in American Historiography,* ed. William T. Hutchinson. Chicago: University of Chicago Press, 1937. Extremely perceptive study of Turner.

————. "Frederick Jackson Turner and the Frontier Approach." University of Kansas City *Review* XVIII (Autumn, 1951), 3–17. Useful study of Turner's methods.

————. "Frederick Jackson Turner, Historian." *Wisconsin Magazine of History* XXV (June, 1942), 408–24. Helpful study of Turner by one of his outstanding students.

————. "Turner Theories and the South." *Journal of Southern History* V (August, 1939), 291–314. Interesting application of the theory in a nonwestern area.

CURTI, MERLE. "The Democratic Theme in American Historical Literature." *Mississippi Valley Historical Review* XXXIX (June, 1952), 3–28. A stimulating essay.

————. "The Section and the Frontier in American History: The Methodological Concepts of Frederick Jackson Turner." In *Methods in Social Science*, ed. Stuart A. Rice. Chicago: University of Chicago Press, 1931. Extremely helpful study of Turner's methods.

DALE, EDWARD EVERETT. "Memoirs of Frederick Jackson Turner." *Mississippi Valley Historical Review* XXX (December, 1943), 339–58. Provides insights into Turner's success as a teacher.

Dial XV (August 1, 1893), 60–61. Gives program of American Historical Association meeting at Chicago.

ELKINS, STANLEY AND ERIC MCKITRICK. "A Meaning for Turner's Frontier." *Political Science Quarterly* LIX (September, December, 1954), 321–53, 565–602. Useful study which supports the thesis.

Extra Census Bulletin No. 12, April 20, 1891. Early statement of the "end of the frontier."

FOERSTER, NORMAN. "American Literature." *Saturday Review of Literature* II (April 3, 1926), 677–79. Helpful discussion of trends in literature.

GOODRICH, CARTER AND SOL DAVISON. "The Frontier As a Safety-Valve: A Rejoinder." *Political Science Quarterly* LIII (June, 1938), 268–71. Helpful in understanding the attack on the safety-valve aspect of the frontier.

————. "The Wage-Earner in the Westward Movement." *Political Science Quarterly* L (June, 1935), 161–85. Useful study of the role of the wage earner in the movement of the frontier.

————. "The Wage-Earner in the Westward Movement." *Political Science Quarterly* LI (March, 1936), 61–116. Continuation of the study of the wage earner in relation to the frontier.

GRESSLEY, GENE M. "The Turner Thesis—A Problem in Historiography." *Agricultural History* XXXII (October, 1958), 227–49. Model essay in historiography; indispensible to any study of the frontier thesis and the arguments advanced both for and against it.

HACKER, LOUIS M. "Sections or Classes." *The Nation* CXXXVII (July 26, 1933), 108–10. Helpful discussion of the sectional theme.

HAYES, CARLTON J. H. "American Frontier—Frontier of What?" *American Historical Review* LI (January, 1946), 199–210. Expresses concern about overemphasis on the study of frontier history.

HEXTER, JACK H. "Review of Walter P. Webb's *The Great Frontier*." *American Historical Review* LVIII (July, 1953), 963. Valuable review of this important book.

HICKS, JOHN D. "Review of Walter P. Webb's *The Great Frontier*." *Saturday Review of Literature* XXXV (December 27, 1952), 10. Helpful examination of Webb's book.

HOCKETT, HOMER C. "Review of Ray A. Billington's *Westward Expansion*." *Mississippi Valley Historical Review* XXXVI (December, 1949), 550–52. Helpful review.

HOFSTADTER, RICHARD. "Turner and the Frontier Myth." *American Scholar* XVIII (October, 1949), 433–43. A provocative essay.

JACOBS, WILBUR R. "Frederick Jackson Turner—Master Teacher." *Pacific Historical Review* XXIII (February, 1954), 49–58. Particularly useful study of Turner as teacher.

———. "Wilson's First Battle at Princeton: The Chair for Turner." *Harvard Library Bulletin* VIII (1954), 74–87. Interesting discussion of Wilson's attempt to secure a chair in history for his friend.

KANE, MURRAY. "Some Considerations on the Frontier Concept of Frederick Jackson Turner." *Mississippi Valley Historical Review* XXVII (December, 1940), 379–400. Extremely interesting discussion.

———. "Some Considerations on the Safety-Valve Doctrine." *Mississippi Valley Historical Review* XXIII (September, 1936), 169–88. Stimulating discussion of the safety-valve concept.

KELLOGG, LOUISE PHELPS. "The Passing of a Great Teacher—Frederick Jackson Turner." *Historical Outlook* XXIII (October, 1932), 270–72. Useful recollection of Turner by one of his students.

LAMAR, HOWARD W. "Frederick Jackson Turner." In *Pastmasters: Some Essays on American Historians,* ed. Marcus Cunliffe and Robin W. Winks. New York: Harper and Row, 1969. Professor Lamar's essay is not only perceptive and informative but an excellent example of prose writing at its best.

LYND, STAUGHTON. "On Turner, Beard and Slavery." *Journal of Negro History* XLVIII (October, 1963), 235–50. Explores an interesting viewpoint.

MEANY, EDMOND S. "The Towns of the Pacific Northwest Were Not Founded on the Fur Trade." American Historical Association, *Annual Report,* 1909. Washington: Government Printing Office, 1911. This article, by one of Turner's students, marked the beginning of the criticism of the frontier thesis.

"The Meeting of the American Historical Association at Indianapolis." *American Historical Review* XVI (April, 1911), 453–75. Covers the annual meeting at which Turner presided as president of the Association; mentions the testimonial dinner given for Turner by his former students.

MIKESELL, MARVIN W. "Comparative Studies in Frontier History." Association of American Geographers, *Annals* L (March, 1960), 62–74. Helpful study of frontier history in various parts of the world.

MOOD, FULMER. "The Development of Frederick Jackson Turner As a Thinker." *Publications of the Colonial Society of Massachusetts, Transactions* XXXIV (December, 1943), 281–352. Extremely informative.

MORISON, SAMUEL E. "Frederick Jackson Turner (1861–1932)." American Academy of Arts and Sciences, *Proceedings* LXVIII (1933), 685–86. Graceful appreciation of Turner.

NETTELS, CURTIS. "Frederick Jackson Turner and the New Deal." *Wisconsin Magazine of History* XVII (March, 1934), 257–65. Interesting and provocative essay.

OSTRANDER, GILMAN M. "Turner and the Germ Theory." *Agricultural History* XXXII (October, 1958), 258–61. Indicates Turner's reliance upon the germ theory.

PARISH, JOHN CARL. "The Persistence of the Westward Movement." *Yale Review* XV (April, 1926), 461–77. Stimulating essay.

PHILLIPS, ULRICH BONNELL. "Memorial to Frederick Jackson Turner." American Historical Association, *Annual Report*, 1932, p. 550. Washington: Government Printing Office, 1933. Indicates some of Turner's contributions to the profession.

————. "The Traits and Contributions of Frederick Jackson Turner." *Agricultural History* XIX (January, 1945), 21–23. Excellent material on Turner's contributions.

PIERSON, GEORGE W. "American Historians and the Frontier Thesis in 1941." *Wisconsin Magazine of History* XXVI (September, December, 1942), 36–60, 170–85. Evaluation of the status of the thesis among historians in 1941.

————. "The Frontier and American Institutions—A Criticism of the Turner Theory." *New England Quarterly* XV (June, 1942), 224–55. Sharply critical of the Turner thesis.

————. "The Frontier and the Frontiersmen of Turner's Essays." *Pennsylvania Magazine of History and Biography* LXIV (October, 1940), 449–78. Criticism of the Turner thesis.

————. "Recent Studies of Turner and the Frontier Doctrines." *Mississippi Valley Historical Review* XXXIV (December, 1947). 453–58. Helpful survey of the continuing discussion of the Turner thesis.

ROBBINS, ROY M. "Review of *The United States 1830–1850: The Nation and Its Sections.*" *Mississippi Valley Historical Review* XXII (September, 1935), 295–97. Helpful review of an important book.

SCHAFER, JOSEPH. "Turner's America." *Wisconsin Magazine of History* XVII (June, 1934), 447–65. Interesting essay by one of Turner's students.

————. "Turner's Early Writing." *Wisconsin Magazine of History* XVI (June, 1933), 213–31. Valuable discussion.

————. "Turner's Frontier Philosophy," *Wisconsin Magazine of History* XVI (June, 1933), 451–69. Helpful exposition of Turner's philosophy.

SCHLESINGER, ARTHUR M. "The City in American History." *Mississippi Valley Historical Review* XXVII (June, 1940), 43–67. Schlesinger states his urban frontier concept; extremely significant essay.

SHANNON, FRED A. "The Homestead Act and the Labor Surplus." *American Historical Review* XLI (July, 1936), 637–52. Excellent critical study.

————. "A Post Mortem on the Labor-Safety-Valve Theory." *Agricultural*

History XIX (January, 1945), 31–38. Further views on the safety-valve theory.

SIMLER, NORMAN J. "The Safety Valve Doctrine Re-Evaluated." *Agricultural History* XXXII (October, 1958), 250–57. Continues the debate over the safety-valve idea.

SUSMAN, WARREN I. "The Useless Past: American Intellectuals and the Frontier Thesis: 1910–1930." *Bucknell Review* II (March, 1963), 1–20. Survey of writings on the frontier.

WILLIAMS, WILLIAM A. "The Frontier Thesis and American Foreign Policy." *Pacific Historical Review* XXV (November, 1955), 379–95. Explores an interesting aspect of the thesis.

WILSON, WOODROW. "The Making of the Nation." *Atlantic Monthly,* LXXX (July, 1897), 1–14. Presents views on the development of the nation.

———. "The Proper Perspective of American History." *Forum* XIX (July, 1895), 544–49. Short, helpful essay.

WINTHER, OSCAR O. "The Frontier Hypothesis and the Historian." *Social Education* XXI (November, 1957), 294–98. Brief, helpful essay.

WRIGHT, BENJAMIN F. "American Democracy and the Frontier." *Yale Review* XX (December, 1930), 349–65. Stimulating essay.

———. "Political Institutions and the Frontier." In *Sources of Culture in the Middle West,* ed. Dixon R. Fox. New York: Appleton-Century, 1934. Helpful study.

———. "Review of Frederick J. Turner's *Significance of Sections in American History.*" *New England Quarterly* VI (September, 1933), 630–34. Valuable review.

Index